WOULD YOU BE WELL?

Clare McKenna has worked as a broadcaster in TV and radio for over twenty-five years.

She began presenting Newstalk's health and wellness show *Alive and Kicking* in 2019 and this sparked an exploration into her own relationship with her wellbeing. After embarking on a deep dive for the show and a national newspaper, Clare began to move away from the clutches of diet culture towards a life where a healthy relationship with food and body was prioritised and, in turn, so was her wellbeing. Impassioned to share this message with others Clare went on to become an Integrative Health Coach to promote lifestyle and preventative medicine. She now hosts events championing individualised wellbeing in small achievable steps, cutting through the noise and overwhelm to empower people to feel as good as they can for as long as they can. Clare is also a master breathwork teacher.

Instagram & Tiktok: @claremckennapresents

www.wouldyoubewell.ie
www.nourishyourself.ie

CLARE MCKENNA

Would You Be WELL?

HACHETTE
BOOKS
IRELAND

Copyright © 2026 Clare McKenna

The right of Clare McKenna to be identified as the author of the work has been asserted by her in accordance with the Copyright, Designs and Patents Act 1988.

First published in Ireland in 2026 by HACHETTE BOOKS IRELAND

1

All rights reserved. No part of this publication may be reproduced, stored in a retrieval system or transmitted, in any form or by any means without the prior written permission of the publisher, nor be otherwise circulated in any form of binding or cover other than that in which it is published and without a similar condition being imposed on the subsequent purchaser.

Illustrations by Bookends Publishing Services and Cathal O'Gara.

Cataloguing in Publication Data is available from the British Library.

ISBN 9781399751810

Typeset in Garamond by Bookends Publishing Services, Dublin.
Printed and bound in Great Britain by Clays Ltd, Elcograf S.p.A.

Hachette Books Ireland policy is to use papers that are natural, renewable and recyclable products and made from wood grown in sustainable forests. The logging and manufacturing processes are expected to conform to the environmental regulations of the country of origin.

Hachette Books Ireland
8 Castlecourt Centre
Castleknock
Dublin 15, Ireland
(info@hbgi.ie)

Authorised representative in the EEA.

A division of Hachette UK Ltd
Carmelite House, 50 Victoria Embankment, London EC4Y 0DZ

www.hachettebooksireland.ie

To my dad, Patrick Joseph McKenna, who taught me that a life well lived is one that is filled with love and laughter

CONTENTS

Before We Start   1
Introduction   3
My Health-and-Wellness Story   7
What Is Wellness?   17
Finding Your Foundation   23
   Burnout   26
   Lifestyle medicine   31
   Blue zones   34
   My foundation   37

Part 1: Mind
Flick the Switch: The mindset shift   45
   Neuroplasticity: change is possible   49
The Stories We Tell Ourselves   55
Negativity Bias   65
   Imposter syndrome   67
   The learning zone   70
   The mindset tools   72
   Mindfulness and meditation   75

Doing the Work   *87*
    Finding the therapist who is right for you   *96*
Show Up for Yourself   *99*
    Take action   *101*
Listen to the Whispers and the Rage   *107*
Can I Say 'No'?   *111*

Part 2: Body
At War With Your Body   *121*
    Interoception   *124*
Dieting Doesn't Work   *127*
Holding In Your Tummy   *137*
Senses and Sensuality   *147*
Eat Up   *151*
    Fruit and veg   *155*
    Protein   *155*
    Carbs   *156*
    Fats   *156*
Gut Health   *161*
Movement   *167*
Rest and Recharge   *173*
    The red-light district   *174*
    Wearable tech   *180*
    Forest bathing   *183*
Sleep Hygiene Tips   *189*
Just Breathe   *191*

Part 3: Soul

Meaning and Purpose   205

Speak Up   207

   Speak up for your health   214

   Speak up for others   215

Doing Things You Think You Can't   217

Sage the Room   225

   The Celtic Wheel   231

Nature   233

   Mooning   235

   Tree hugging   236

Living Your Best Life   239

Do You Believe in Magic?   245

Life-Coach Cynic   251

Connection   259

Joy   267

Let's Have a Recap   273

   Holiday you   279

   What to keep an eye on   281

   And most importantly – tune in   290

Exercises   295

   Strengths exercise   295

   Values exercise   296

   The Circle of Life tool   298

Bibliography   303

Acknowledgements   308

At the end of some chapters, you'll find questions to help you reflect on your wellbeing. Feel free to just think about these questions as you go through your day – though I would also recommend having a journal and pen to hand to record your answers.

BEFORE WE START

Before we get going, I wanted to take a moment to say that this book is intended to be fully inclusive and meet you where you are at. We are all unique. We will delve into this in more detail throughout the book but I want you to know that no assumptions have been made about you. This is a book for everyone regardless of how you identify, your life stage, neurodiversity or ability. It is my belief that everyone deserves to feel as well as they can for as long as they can, whatever that looks like to them. So, if I mention movement, and, for you, that means stretching from your chair then that is just as powerful as the person who heads out for a run (this is not me!). When I mention getting still and focusing on your thoughts, if you are neurodivergent this is going to be more challenging than if you are neurotypical – find a way that works best for you. If I talk about finding a GP you can trust, that can be challenging based on where you live or your financial situation, and certain communities can find it more difficult to access the healthcare they need. I am aware of all of this as I write.

My intention is that whoever you are or wherever you are at in your life stage, that you will find what works for you, take what you need from this book and leave the rest. There really is no right or wrong way to be healthy or well; tying yourself in knots trying to live up to a standard of what you *should* be doing is the very opposite of what you are trying to achieve. Go gentle but have the courage to reach for the life and the wellbeing you deserve. Let the starting point be that you are incredible just as you are now and anything you bring into your life to improve your wellbeing is an added bonus.

Now, let's go ...

INTRODUCTION

I didn't hit rock bottom.

I didn't have a difficult diagnosis or find myself thousands of euro in debt. Instead, I moved through life taking on all the health and wellness trends that came my way until I couldn't take on anymore. I was exhausted, overwhelmed and unmotivated. I wanted to write this book for people like me, people who want to feel and look their best but who are so bombarded by the health-and-wellness machine that they don't know where to start.

After being sold the theory of 'no pain, no gain', I thought that feeling exhausted mentally and physically was par for the course when it came to living your best life. If you're not pushing yourself to be the best version of yourself then are you truly living?

Having so many health-and-wellness messages coming at us can lead to a cycle of not knowing where to start – and guilt for not starting at all. If you do start, it's with all guns blazing, only to find sustaining this new world order is impossible and the guilt cycle begins again. This is where I found myself about six years ago and it had been going on for most of my adult life.

We have access to so much more information today, which can have its advantages but it can also be overwhelming. Conflicting advice, the deluge of 'experts' ... the sheer volume of it can wear you down. My hope with this book is that rather than adding to the overload, I can help you to cut through that overwhelm and create a health-and-wellness plan that works for you.

Over the past six years I have focused on my own health and wellbeing, studied the area extensively and received several qualifications, and through my work have interviewed hundreds of experts and heard real-life stories of illness and overcoming. What all of this has taught me is that it really is the simple things that matter the most (we'll delve into these in the book). But simplicity doesn't mean easy, and bringing change to your life can be challenging.

The wellness industry makes us think that we can only be healthy if we are ticking a multitude of boxes all at once. From juicing to meditating to pushing our bodies to the max. Ice baths and saunas, oxygen chambers and salt caves. The 5 a.m. clubs and the lists of what successful people do, just reading them would exhaust you. I'm here to tell you that you are entitled to choose what makes *you* feel good: this is the essence of wellness. If you never set foot in a cryo chamber but you feel good within yourself and about yourself, you truly are 'living your best life'.

I believe that the main components of a health-and-wellness life are:

- a healthy relationship with your body and food
- good people in your life
- self-worth
- meaning and purpose.

It's not easy to have all of these in check all of the time but I hope it's refreshing that on that list there is no mention of a personal trainer, private chef or Balinese retreat. I would love all three but I now know that a better starting point is to drown out the noise of the wellness world, tune in to what we truly need and take small steps to get there.

I did. I stopped listening to all the 'shoulds' I was told I needed to do to be healthy, and I started to listen to myself – and it has been transformative. Living this way goes far beyond what is on my plate or what the scales say. When you feel better, you make better choices and everything improves.

Wellness endeavours are no longer healthy when it takes unhealthy behaviours to achieve results. You can get there in a slower and a gentler way and – guess what – you're allowed to enjoy it. You don't need rules and discipline but you do need to commit to showing up for yourself through the good, the bad and the ugly that life will throw your way. Your health and wellbeing foundation is there to stabilise and support you, not push you over the edge.

MY HEALTH-AND-WELLNESS STORY

Let me start by telling you a bit about me. I was not a child well versed in health and wellbeing and nor do I think I should have been; childhood is a time for carefree innocence. My dad was a major advocate for team sports, not just for exercise but as a way to meet people and make friends. I liked the friends part but the sport ... not so much. I was practically allergic to PE at school, often sitting out sessions claiming period pain, which seemed to arrive weekly as opposed to monthly. At home, there was always an emphasis on eating well. My mum was and still is a fantastic cook and sitting at the table for all our meals was a family occasion and a tradition I'm still so grateful for today. We would go for walks, head to swimming and dance lessons, I'd cycle around on my bike and I had a lovely childhood free from organised sport. I was more into speech and drama and the debating team – hence the career choice, I suppose.

I grew up in the 1990s and 2000s, a great time in so many ways. Girl power was at an all-time high and, with a booming economy, it really did seem like anything was possible. There was also a rather insidious obsession with the body beautiful – we hadn't yet begun to talk about airbrushing, body positivity or even mental health. Magazines were hugely popular, their pages filled with not only picture-perfect models but also deep dives into weight-loss journeys, and often there was a calling-out of what was considered to be a body flaw – very normal weight gain or cellulite with accompanying photos where the flaw was circled.

Reality TV was beginning its ascent and with it came so-called ordinary people, just like us, shooting to stardom and often with a body transformation, diet plan and workout video to boot. There were several who would then do a tell-all a few months later where they'd confess that the diet plan had all been a con and they had survived on little or no calories in the lead-up to their shoot. We had pop stars talking about maple-syrup-and-cayenne-pepper diets, alongside the marketing of diet shakes, slimming clubs and promises to help you drop a dress size in two weeks.

I was fairly body confident growing up, but all this began to seep in. I began questioning my body shape, and the messaging coming my way seemed to be to cut calories.

My early twenties became entwined with a need to be smaller, faster, thinner, stronger and basically anything I wasn't at the time. Then the gym was introduced to the calorie-counting and my body began to change. When I left school, I discovered the gym for the first time and I loved it. Competing with just me and losing myself in a class or a weight session became a non-negotiable, and I enjoyed the feeling of building strength and achieving targets. I liked the discipline, the goal-setting, the sense of achievement, but I gave no thought to the impact it was having on my long-term health.

I was working full-time in a nine-to-five job, at college studying part-time at night, had a restaurant job at the weekend and still found time to party with my friends. I cared little for home-cooked meals, surviving mainly on brown toast and chocolate spread, takeaway noodles and heading home for the odd 'Mammy dinner'.

A major life change came when at the age of twenty-one I started working for an internet company, one of the first in Ireland. I loved that job, and made friends for life, and they really invested in their staff. We had social events and trips away, as well as lots of opportunity, but it was the personal-development courses they sent us on that were a real game-changer for me.

I sat in the audience at motivational talks, hearing for the first time about creating your dream life. We had workshops on goal-setting and the idea of intentional living, figuring out what you truly wanted and going for it.

The internet was only beginning at that time so access to this language and information wasn't as easy as it is now. There were no memes or podcasts, no gurus to follow on social media. There were books, of course, but I hadn't read any of them and from the stage, speakers told of humble beginnings and now mansions and yachts. It was often about making money but these talks introduced me to concepts such as self-reflection, writing down your goals and the power of a positive mindset. I went all in.

I became renowned in my friendship and work circles for being into health and wellness. I went to every class, every discipline, retreat and personal-development course. I was never without a bottle of water by my side, brought cooked chicken breasts to work, drank nettle tea and had a collection of supplements that would rival any pharmacy. I read the books, wrote the vision board and followed every dieting trend from macrobiotic to juicing, Atkins to paleo.

And the trends were coming so thick and fast that I couldn't keep up or stay consistent. I was swinging from plant-based to carnivore, depending on what I'd read or seen that week. My compliance to each trend was getting trickier and, let's not forget, I was trying to 'do it all' on a limited calorie intake and with a punishing exercise regime.

But life was good as I moved through my twenties and into my thirties. I was happily married, had two babies and the greatest of friends and family. My career was flying too – I had moved from the nine-to-five world to the on-air world (more on this later) and when the opportunity to present Newstalk's health-and-wellness show came my way I jumped at the chance. I saw myself as someone who was into health and wellness but what I didn't realise then was that I was actually driven by fads. I was looking to outside sources to tell me what I *should* be doing and I had stopped listening to myself.

In the early days of the show, I remember a moment on air when I had performance nutritionist Daniel Davey on to talk about his first book, *Eat Up*. He spoke about health in a very different way to what I was used to. He was talking about lean muscle mass, not as a desired aesthetic but as a key indicator of long-term health and predisposition to disease. It was a lightbulb moment for me: I still had a way to go and lots of unpicking to do, but it was in that moment that I admitted to myself that I was exhausted. I had tied myself up in knots trying to do everything right, and I had allowed unhealthy habits to become part of my everyday – food guilt, dieting, pushing through instead of prioritising rest, and allowing negative self-talk.

I realised there must be more people like me, feeling confused and overwhelmed with health and wellness. I decided to embark on a challenge to explore the topic in depth. Health and wellness was the theme of the radio show and I realised that I wasn't 100 per cent certain about what that truly meant.

I gathered a group of experts to help me on my quest. Daniel Davey had to be there on nutrition and mindset. Claire McGrath and Rosie Harte, former bodybuilders who were coaching people to repair their relationship with their body and food. Andy Ramage, author of *Let's Do This*, on the psychology of motivation and behaviour change. And Paul and Fiona Oppermann of Dublin Sports Clinic on the most effective way to build lean muscle.

At the beginning, I was still so tied up in body image and diet culture that it was mainly the 'lean muscle' part that spoke to me and I couldn't wait to get to the end of the challenge where I would flex my new muscles and tell everyone how I got there.

However, over the course of a year, I had a complete turn in focus that took me by surprise. My attention shifted from how I looked to how I felt. I began to look at my relationship with my body and food as well as the power of small, consistent steps. I threw away food rules and began to eat balanced meals that included all food groups; this gave me more headspace and so much more energy. In turn, I was more up for moving my body, I was sleeping better and I was feeling great.

The original plan had been to do the challenge over six months, talk about it on the radio and write about it in a Sunday paper – but then the pandemic hit, putting a halt to all of our gallops. I had never really experienced anxiety before; I'd had anxious moments and stressful times but this was the first time that I felt prolonged levels of fear over what might happen. Feeling this way and having the enforced slower pace of life gave me a chance to lean in to all the mental-health strategies I'd been hearing about for so long and to truly feel the benefits.

Terrified of the unknown, stressed to the max with home-schooling and trying to keep it all together, I started meditating, doing online yoga, breathwork and a mindfulness course. And they really helped. After each one, I would feel calmer and slightly more in control. The situation hadn't changed – in fact it went from bad to worse as we navigated lockdowns and my dad's dementia plummeted – but my reactions to the situation changed. I had started to strengthen myself within the chaos around me.

At the end of the challenge, which had become my health-and-wellness year, I emerged with better energy levels, better mental health and better health outcomes for my future – and it had all come down to very simple things. I had shifted my mindset from punishing to nourishing and I felt better for it. I realised that I'd let the wellness industry begin to make me feel unwell; now the power was in my hands once more and I wasn't going back.

I went on to qualify as an integrative health coach, learning about lifestyle and preventative medicine, and I began sharing what I'd learnt with others via events and online courses.

We lead such busy lives, and wellness can become something we feel we just don't have time for. The messaging can make us feel that we are not good enough or doing enough. It's no wonder we want to bury ourselves under the duvet and stay there.

Now, I want to share what I've learnt even more widely and hope it will empower you to create a plan that is right for you, in the life that you have right now. That you let go of the 'shoulds' and begin to listen to yourself about what living at your best means to you. That you move from self-criticism to self-compassion and begin to nourish yourself – mind, body and soul.

I hope you will laugh at some of the adventures I've been on and the mistakes I've made. We can get so caught up in the seriousness and the judgement, and there really is no need for it.

I hope you will have a major mindset shift, like I did, and realise that to be successful, it doesn't need to be hard. You deserve to feel as good as you can for as long as you can.

And if you are someone who feels they've got health and wellness down, then let this be a chance to check back in, see what's changed and how else you can best support yourself. I often need a reset reminder.

I've divided the book into three sections:
1. Mind
2. Body
3. Soul.

Beginning to think of your health in this way is the first step. We aren't robots, you can't just fuel us up and send us off. We are complex, emotional beings and we need to start thinking beyond just physical health. Throughout each section, we'll look at various practices and themes so you can get a greater understanding of each and, from there, decide what works for you.

I've also included a number of practical sessions with questions for you to work through. Remember to go easy on yourself throughout and have fun with this. We are all doing the best we can with what we've got, but there is always an opportunity to start afresh.

Change can be challenging but it is easier with support. When you begin to back yourself, that's truly the best support there is.

WHAT IS WELLNESS?

Health and wellness looks different for everyone because we are all unique. What works for me may not work for you, there is no one-size-fits-all approach.

We currently have a crisis-model healthcare system: we wait for something to go wrong before we ask for help. Thankfully, we have begun to talk more about preventative and lifestyle medicine, looking at how we live and how it impacts our health. This should be empowering rather than imply the notion of blame that says that if you get sick, it must have been something you've done or not done – and that simply isn't correct. People will get sick, it is a difficult but natural part of life.

Wellness has become a multitrillion euro empire, and it can cause groaning eye rolls as many consider it to be made-up nonsense designed to help silly people spend their money. The term was first used in the 1950s by Dr Halbert L.

Dunn (globalwellnessinstitute.org). He defined wellness as the relationship between our abilities and our environment, moving beyond the simple absence of illness to encompass a more holistic view of wellbeing.

The *Oxford English Dictionary* definition of wellness is a 'condition obtained when a person achieves a level of health that minimises their chances of getting sick'. Isn't that what we're all hoping to do? Minimise the chances of serious illness so we can live as healthily as we can for as long as we can? The *OED* goes on to say: 'Wellness is achieved by a combination of emotional, environmental, mental, physical, social and spiritual health.'

Wellness isn't a fad, some made-up mumbo jumbo to line the pockets of conglomerates – although it has been hijacked to do so. It's a way of living that, when harnessed correctly and with flexibility, can help you feel at your best and fortify you at your worst through the normal ebb and flow of life.

I believe in you, I'm backing you – now let's dive in.

WELL? OVER TO YOU ...

Let's start with looking at where you are and where you would like to be.

Remember, there are no right or wrong answers here but, hopefully, by considering these questions, you will begin to shed light on areas that need attention and where tweaks might help your life flow better.

Use a 1 to 10 scale (where 1 is 'not great' and 10 is 'great') to answer the following questions.

How do you feel today?

How good do you feel about yourself?

What areas of your life cause you most stress?

What in life brings you the most joy?

How often do you put yourself first?

What do you do to relax?

Which of the following areas of your life need attention?
- Food
- Movement
- Stress management
- Career
- Relationships
- Rest
- Fun
- Sleep

When do you feel most at peace?

What do you do for fun?

What in your life is not serving you anymore?

If you could change one thing about your life, what would it be?

If money was no object, what would you do with your life?

Do you believe in yourself to achieve what you set your mind to?

What are some of the obstacles in your way?

What's top of your list when it comes to your wellbeing? (Something you prioritise now or something you would like to.)

When something doesn't work out as you intended, do you blame yourself?

How often do you speak negatively to yourself?

FINDING YOUR FOUNDATION

We all know that to build a decent house that lasts, you need a solid foundation – well, it's the same when it comes to our wellbeing. Taking the time to work out what gives me a solid base has meant that I know when I've gone off-track and what I need to do to get back to feeling good again. A strong foundation also helps you to weather what life throws at you as you've built a personalised toolbox of coping skills that you can lean on.

Taking the time to figure out what works for you is not a quick fix – rather, it's an investment in yourself and while it will need constant tweaking as life evolves, your wellness foundation is there to strengthen you and make life flow with more ease.

As we get thrown curveballs or move through difficult seasons in our lives, it's completely understandable that we will 'fall off the wagon', gathering scrapes and bruises as we career into the nearest ditch. During these times we may turn to the things that give us comfort, that make us feel safe, even if some of these things don't serve us in the long term. I'm talking alcohol, late nights, fast food, bad relationships, procrastination – there is a place for all of these (mainly the food, alcohol and late nights) but if we stay in these comforts for too long, they begin to wear us down.

Going off-track can creep up on you; you might not even notice it until you are on the floor. Getting started again is challenging and will require the most effort. The optimum setup is to know yourself so well that you can catch it and get back on track earlier. It's important that we don't demonise any behaviours – we don't go from 'being' bad to 'being' good, instead we go from 'feeling' low to feeling 'good'.

Here are some of the indications that things may be on the slide:

- You snap more and have less patience and tolerance for everyday situations.
- You feel you have little energy for the tasks at hand.
- You wake up tired despite having slept the night before.
- You feel an unusual sense of dread about work and even social commitments.
- You find it challenging to believe in yourself and to be optimistic.

- Your digestive system is off.
- You experience physical symptoms, such as headaches or tension in your neck and shoulders.
- You find yourself reaching more often for stimulants, such as caffeine and sugar, to prop you up and get you through.
- You are leaning on unhealthy substances, such as alcohol, to manage stress and wind down.
- You fall into bed at night but find it difficult to get to sleep and often wake during the night.

The reason I know that these things should be included in this list is because I have experienced every single one of them – and still do from time to time. The difference today is that instead of just seeing them as the way things are or just who I am, I now look at them as messages, little battle cries from my body that war is about to break out if I don't address the situation.

Each thing on the list is an indication that you have given out too much energy without replenishing your mental, physical and emotional stores, and while I'm no mathematician, I think we all understand that you can't keep making withdrawals without making deposits.

I heard an interview with the incredible Dr Joe Dispenza and he talked about what happens when our brain is completely overloaded and burned out: we feel stressed, frustrated and angry. Now, aren't those three states of mind we are seeing a lot in the world today?

Chronic stress – when stress becomes simply the backdrop to how we live – is associated with inflammation in the body and this can lead to all kinds of health issues. Humans are amazingly resilient and we will adapt to almost any situation, but this can lead to us normalising constant stress. Many of us live feeling five out of ten (or less) without even realising it, and without knowing how to turn up that dial to experience how good life could really feel.

Burnout

When it comes to burnout, often we think of the person who literally can't get out of bed, whose systems have broken down and who needs interventions and time to come back to themselves. This is, indeed, a true representation, but what we don't talk about as often are the steps that lead to this breaking point.

The twelve stages of burnout, as identified by Herbert Freudenberger & Gail North (1992), describe a progressive decline in wellbeing and performance due to chronic stress.

These stages are:
1. **Compulsion to prove oneself:** Feeling the need to constantly demonstrate worth.
2. **Working harder:** Driven to put in excessive effort, often at the expense of personal needs.

3. **Neglecting needs**: Prioritising work over sleep, eating well and social interaction.
4. **Displacement of conflicts**: Stress is directed outwards, often towards loved ones or colleagues.
5. **Revision of values**: Work becomes the sole focus, with other aspects of life devalued.
6. **Denial of problems**: Ignoring or minimising the negative impacts of stress and fatigue.
7. **Withdrawal**: Social isolation and a decline in hobbies and interests.
8. **Odd behavioural changes**: Noticeable shifts in personality and behaviour.
9. **Depersonalisation**: Feeling detached and disconnected from oneself and others.
10. **Inner emptiness**: Experiencing a profound sense of void and lack of motivation.
11. **Depression**: Feelings of exhaustion, hopelessness, and despair.
12. **Burnout syndrome**: Complete physical and mental exhaustion, potentially leading to collapse.

Stage 3, when you start neglecting your own needs and self-care, is where I hope you will catch yourself. Of course, stages 1 and 2 would be good to avoid too but we live in a society that promotes busyness and productivity so it's easy to get caught up in it.

We all have dreams, aspirations and responsibilities but they shouldn't cost you your health. Finding your self-worth outside of what you do and prioritising your own needs is essential – realising this is a major turning point in strengthening your foundation and wellbeing. You know the safety drill on the plane: you attend to your own oxygen mask first and this enables you to do everything else much better and it can save your life.

WELL? OVER TO YOU ...

Now, where are you at with burnout? Answer these questions.

How often do you put the needs of others ahead of your own? (Use a scale of 1 to 10 where 1 is 'never' and 10 is 'all of the time'.)

Who or what do you prioritise in life? (Write down every one, there are unavoidable and much-loved responsibilities, such as family, work and pets, but it is worth being aware of where your attention is going before you can work out how to include yourself on this list.)

How much do you value others' opinions?

Do you seek the praise and validation of others? If so, why?

Who do you want to make the most proud of you in life?

What do you think it means to be a 'good' person?

What do you need in life to make it flow at its best?

WOULD YOU BE WELL?

How are your energy levels day to day? (Use a scale of 1 to 10 where 1 is 'extremely low' and 10 is 'extremely high'.)

How do you feel when you wake up in the morning?

How do you feel when you get to the end of the day and bedtime?

What do you spend most of your day doing?

Do you enjoy this?

Does self-care feature in your life?

What does self-care mean for you? Are there moments in your day, week or month that you could dedicate just to you?

Are there tweaks you could make to your life to help it to flow better?

Lifestyle medicine

When we reach the edges of burnout, when we begin to feel utterly depleted, it can be difficult to see the wood for the trees, and to see a logical way back. The best way to get back to where you want to be is by taking small and gentle steps, but that's not the story we are sold.

We are sold the quick fix, the overnight transformation. We are told 'no pain, no gain' and while making changes in our lives requires effort, if it comes at great cost to our mental health and overall sense of wellbeing, then how can it possibly be healthy?

Lifestyle medicine is now evidence based, with many studies looking at the way we live and how that affects how we feel.

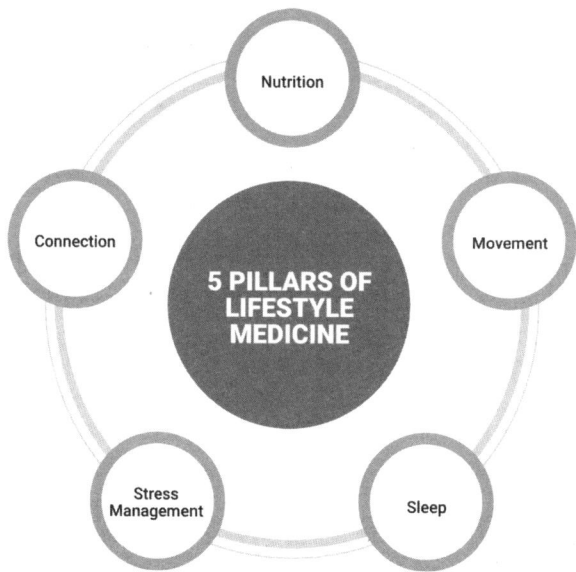

Figure 1: The five pillars of lifestyle medicine

You will see different iterations of lifestyle medicine but they all emphasise the importance of how we are living and the impact this has on how we feel.

So often in the health message, the focus is on diet and exercise alone. When I was training as a health coach, we learnt the concept of primary and secondary foods – the importance of how we are living being primary and what is on our plate being secondary. You can fill your plate with as many greens as it can hold but if you are stressed out in your worklife and your relationships, it will be more challenging to feel the benefits of the nutrition. Chronic stress impacts our central nervous system, and as all our systems are interconnected, it impairs how we feel – our energy levels, our immune system and our mood.

You might be doing what I was – spending so much time focusing on food and exercise that you don't think about the importance of connection, your sleep or managing your finances. Or perhaps you are overthinking it, a ball of worry about the data on your REM sleep. Start by dropping perfection-striving. Accept that life is marvellous but messy and just focus on doing the best you can.

It's important to look at these pillars when building our foundation: nutrition, movement, sleep, stress management and connection – if one or more of them is off-kilter then we will be too. Take a look at what is contributing to your stress levels, perhaps stopping you from getting a good night's sleep. Is it your workload? Is it the season of life you are in? Is it because you aren't making time for yourself? Are you tech heavy and nature starved? Are you eating well to give you the energy you need?

Knowing where you are is the first step to getting where you want to be.

After considering these things, ask yourself what small steps you can take to bring some balance back to your life. How can you better care for yourself? What is it that you need?

'Balance' is an interesting and somewhat dangerous word. It conjures up an image of a scales where everything is even, a work–life ideal that I don't believe exists. It is all just life: regardless of your work situation, be it in an office, in hospitality, in a factory or a caring role, there isn't a time when you have everything nailed and put the exact same energy into each part of your life as the perfect worker, family member, friend or partner – it's a myth.

Where do you feature in all of this? Where are your needs being met? We can often wait for time to just land in our lap and then we'll meditate, head out to the woods or meet a friend for a coffee. But that time doesn't just land, it needs to be mapped out and prioritised like a work meeting or dental appointment (but more fun).

While goals are important, the best approach is to avoid

focusing on a destination point, thinking *I'll be happy when ...* Instead, stay in the here and now with the small steps you can take every day to create a foundation that works best for you.

Blue zones

In the blue zones around the world, the places where people live the longest and healthiest, it is the simplest of things that make the biggest difference.

The blue zones include:

- **Okinawa, Japan**: Known for its strong emphasis on social connections and plant-based diets – grains, legumes, fruits and vegetables.
- **Sardinia, Italy**: Features a strong family structure and a culture of regular, moderate physical activity – think walking and wood-chopping.
- **Nicoya Peninsula, Costa Rica**: Known for its focus on family, faith and a sense of purpose.
- **Ikaria, Greece**: Celebrated for its Mediterranean diet and lifestyle – grains, fish and lean meats, fresh fruits and vegetables, legumes, all locally sourced.
- **Loma Linda, California**: A community of Seventh Day Adventists whose culture promotes a plant-based diet, regular physical activity, a strong sense of community and faith, including strict adherence to principles like not smoking or drinking alcohol.

National Geographic reporter Dan Buettner and his team have been instrumental in bringing the Blue Zones to public consciousness through his books, *The Blue Zones* and *The Blue Zones Solution*, and Netflix documentaries. They cross-referenced each Blue Zone to create a definitive list of lifestyle practices. They include:

- **Natural movement**: People in Blue Zones are often physically active in their daily routines, such as gardening and walking the fields, and these activities are consistent and feature almost every day. They do not use personal trainers or have fancy gym memberships or equipment.
- **Purpose**: Having a sense of purpose in life is linked to longevity and wellbeing.
- **Downshift**: Managing stress through practices like prayer, meditation or spending time in nature.
- **80 per cent rule**: Eating until they are 80 per cent full, rather than feeling completely stuffed.
- **Plant slant**: A diet rich in plant-based foods like vegetables, fruits, beans and wholegrains.
- **Wine at five**: In some areas, moderate, regular consumption of wine, typically with meals and within community. We're talking a glass of local wine or sake – binge drinking is not a feature.
- **Belonging**: Strong social connections, family ties and a sense of belonging within a community.

- **Right tribe**: Strong social networks and support systems. The Okinawans maintain a powerful social network throughout their lives called a 'moai', a lifelong circle of friends that begins in childhood and meets regularly right into old age. The 'moai' concept originated hundreds of years ago as a way of pooling resources but has become more of a revered social group over time. Traditionally groups of about five young children are grouped together and meet daily or weekly, with some groups lasting over ninety years. Now isn't that a much better health-and-wellbeing way of life than dieting!
- **Loved ones**: Living near or with family, including extended family. Intergenerational living – i.e. with several generations living under the one roof from grandparent to grandchild – is a regular occurrence in many of the Blue Zones. The saying 'it takes a village' is very much a part of our human existence and experience but the modern-day Western way of life has seen a rise in isolation and loneliness.

When we talk about living longer in the Blue Zones, it also means living healthier, with far fewer instances of chronic disease and brain degeneration. The ways of life that aid this longevity are relatively simple, but modern-day society has allowed industry and technology to distance us from these things. But we can bring them back to our own lives, and although this can be challenging and can take time, it will lead to more intentional living. And this is where we want to be.

My foundation

For me, my foundation is (in no particular order):
- Eating balanced meals
- Getting rest
- Moving my body
- Starting my morning slowly – breathwork
- Connecting with people I love.

Do I have this down all the time? No, but when I start to feel off I know it's time to return to my foundation. I book in a date night with my husband, organise some family time or a girls' night out. In the morning, I stop scrolling on Instagram and return to the breathwork or meditation that I know is a much better start for me. I take the time to cook some meals and rein in grabbing food on the go and eating at my desk. I get myself out in nature for a walk in the woods or on the beach, or have a dip in the sea. Simple steps that start bringing me back to myself.

When I'm feeling overwhelmed, weepy and have less patience, I take a look at how I've been living. Often, I'll find I've been working too hard, burning the candle at both ends, scrolling on my phone too much, grabbing a protein bar in a petrol station and calling it lunch. Here and there, these things are fine but, over time, they begin to compound and pull down your energy levels and your mood. By tracking how you feel – your energy levels, your motivation, your mood – and tracing it back to how you've been living gives you the information you need to reset and to do what you need to do to return to your foundation.

WELL? OVER TO YOU ...

What are your foundations?

Are your foundations a part of your daily life? Is one missing from your life completely?

How far away are you from what's missing now?

Do you need to reset your foundation or perhaps set it for the first time?

Remember, we don't need to overthink this. Keep the pillars of lifestyle medicine in your mind to help you build your own foundations – nutrition, movement, sleep, stress management, connection.

Where are you at with the pillars of lifestyle medicine? (Use a scale of 1 to 10 where 1 is 'not good' and 10 is 'brilliant'.)
- Nutrition
- Movement
- Sleep
- Stress management
- Connection

Part 1
MIND

Your mind is a powerful tool but it is only one part of the picture. The conversation around mental health has come a long way in recent years but it's still often seen as a separate entity rather than being interconnected with what else is happening in our lives. We talk about mental health as if it's a bag we carry around with us when, in truth, it is a fully integrated part of who we are.

It goes back to the crisis model of healthcare: we wait for something to go wrong before seeking help. Mental health shouldn't only be considered when there is something wrong; rather, it is there all the time regardless of how we feel. There is still a lot of stigma associated with having mental-health issues and this can make it difficult to put a hand up and admit that you need help. This stigma also perpetuates the idea that these issues are something that happens to someone else rather than all of us, and this can stop us from leaning in to the everyday practices that can make a massive difference.

In this section, we're going to look at some of these practices and examine the various mindsets that might not be serving us on our wellness journey. By acknowledging these, we can slowly learn how to adjust and move out of them, to change the way we think and feel. We'll look at our thoughts and how they influence our habits and behaviours, and the small steps we can take to care for our minds.

FLICK THE SWITCH: THE MINDSET SHIFT

How we think has a major impact on how we feel. One of the biggest changes I hope you will make is to your mindset around health and wellness. Are you ready to flick the switch? To shift your mindset from self-loathing to self-love? Are you ready to set your foundation to one that is nourishing rather than punishing?

Here's how it works: rather than living with rules and restrictions, you make decisions based on what will make you feel well. For example:

- You buy food for the week because you want to set yourself up so that your energy levels are at their best and you want to feel good.
- You head out with your friends for pizza and belly laughs because it's good for the soul.

- You get up and take a morning walk on the beach because it's a great way to clear your head.
- You chill on the couch for an afternoon because rest is important – and you don't feel guilty about it.

An essential component to all of this is that you are kind to yourself, however that looks. For too long, the focus has been on improving or changing your body but it's far more positive to focus on how you feel today and how you want to feel later in life. Don't get me wrong – I like how it feels when I've been consistent with a gym class and I start to see muscle tone or my clothes fitting more comfortably, but this is not my driving force. I've widened my motivation lens to include better mental health, long-term health and improved energy levels. By going to a gym class, I not only get to work out but I also get to connect with friends – we head for a coffee where we talk about the complexities of parenting or whatever the pop-culture news is; it's not all about muscle tone.

I often have weeks where work takes over, eating on the go slips back in and, at the end of the week, my clothes feel a little tighter – this is not a bad week, this is just life.

After a busy week like that, I give myself a reset over the weekend with lots of downtime and I reconnect with my family and then I get back to the things I know make me feel at my best. If those busy weeks were to continue unchecked, I would start to feel sluggish, have brain fog, be more short-tempered and my sleep would be off. So that's why I reset – not because I have to, but because I want to. I feel better when I do.

It can be really helpful to look at your energy levels in a transactional way. So, for everything you give out – be it to work, family, relationships or your community – what are you doing to replenish and top that back up? It doesn't have to be a negative focus necessarily – thinking of all these elements of life draining you – but rather knowing that you will need to rest and recharge your energy levels to enable you to be the best version of yourself as life requires it.

We all have chapters in our lives when things will ramp up – a new job or work project, a new baby, a sick family member, or an illness of our own. Whatever it is, we need to just get through these times as best we can. Leaning on that solid foundation and the pillars – nutrition, movement, sleep, stress management, connection – that hold you up, as discussed on page 31, will not only help as you piece yourself back together but will also help you throughout the challenging times.

During the pandemic, my husband had to face the difficult decision to close the business he had run for twenty years. It was tourism-based and with the closing down of the world, it was just not sustainable to keep it all going. It was a very sad and stressful time for both of us, with the emotions associated with such a life change as well as sorting through all the legal and financial ramifications. I remember speaking about it on my radio show during peak stress. There was so much going on – we had the business closure, my work, our two kids, caring for my dad – and the idea of meditating, going for a walk or cooking a decent meal, even meeting with friends when it was possible to do so, seemed like too much, like it would tip me over the edge. But this was the time I needed my foundation more than ever, I needed to take care of my mind so that I could make it through as best I could. I needed to mind myself so I could mind the people who needed me.

The things we often crave at these times can include alcohol, late nights in front of the television and sleeping in, just getting through it as we struggle to cope. Adding in wellness can seem like a step too far. I know there will be some of you who are solo parenting, caring for a loved one, running a business – whatever the challenge, it can so easily happen that you begin to just go through the motions, eating on the go, not making time to rest or exercise, falling into bed at night only to wake hours later and struggle to get back to sleep.

These are the times when it's essential that we lean in to what makes us feel good – to top ourselves back up, even if it is just a little at a time. In the aftermath of my husband's business closing, as well as being there to support him I had to support myself. Short walks, five-minute meditations, a few deep breaths and making time to sit down and eat a decent meal all helped us to get through it. Together, the tiniest efforts build to make a big difference – three deep breaths before you head into the hospital, a walk around the block just to clear your head, a smoothie or a soup so you know you're getting some fruit and veg in, asking for support for even half an hour so you can do something that is just for you or so you can do absolutely nothing. As we said in the last section, self-care is not selfish, it's a necessity and you need to put yourself first because, when you do, it means you can be the best version of yourself for all the other people and responsibilities on your list.

Neuroplasticity: change is possible

Change can be tricky at the start. Our brains are protection devices that constantly try to spot patterns that will save us energy and keep us safe. That's why learning a new skill requires lots of patience and practice.

Neuroplasticity is the ability of our brains to form and reorganise synaptic connections in response to learning or experience, so we can create new neural pathways – new thought patterns and habits – based on repeating a new behaviour over and over again.

Picture the path you're on as one that is worn down through a grassy field. For years your footsteps have trodden down the grass and created a path and now it's pretty easy to meander along. To start a new path alongside this would be tricky; the grass will be longer and harder to wade through, requiring more effort and taking more time and consistency to match the well-worn path. But, over time, the new path becomes the worn path and the grass grows up on the old path until it's hard to remember where exactly it was. It is the same with your habits. When you take on something new, it takes a lot more effort at the beginning but if you keep tipping away and stay consistent, before you know it, the new path is just the way things are. You go from a change of habit to a change in lifestyle.

WELL? OVER TO YOU ...

What are the healthy habits you could introduce or stay consistent with?

Movement – where will this feature in your day and week?

Eating well – what does this look like for you?

Taking time for yourself – where in your day can you fit this in, even a short few minutes?

What will you do with those minutes?

Can you make a weekly or monthly date with yourself? What will you do?

Where does time in nature feature in your day and week? (The recommended amount for our mental health is two-and-a-half hours per week. This can be broken up into smaller segments.)

Where are you at with stress in your life? (Use a scale of 1 to 10 where 1 is 'rarely experience stress' and 10 is 'stressed all the time'.)

What are the main causes of stress in your life?

What do you do during and after stressful experiences in your life?

Are there changes you could make in your life to reduce the amount of stress you are experiencing?

Can you ask for more support? What would that look like?

How much fun are you having in your life?

Can you revisit a hobby or pastime that you love, or take up a new one?

Can you spend more time with the people who light you up?

How is your sleep? (Use a scale of 1 to 10 where 1 is 'not good at all' and 10 is 'great'.)

Do you have good sleep hygiene? A comfortable bed and bedroom, decent blinds, curtains or an eye mask? Is it a cool and peaceful environment?

Do you make time to wind down before bed? Are there habits you can introduce that will indicate to you and your body that it is time to wind down and prepare for sleep? These could include: a shower or bath, dimming lights or lighting candles, introducing relaxing scents or body oils such as lavender, reading, listening to an audiobook, sleep audio or relaxing music. Or perhaps writing down what you have on your mind or on your to-do list and putting it aside for tomorrow and resigning yourself to rest.

What is your night-time routine?

Where could you make improvements?

What is your relationship with the tech in your life? Smartphones, laptops and even television all have many positives but they can impact on our rest and our sleep – where could you make changes?

Does caffeine impact on your sleep and your rest – could you make changes, such as cutting down or having a cut-off point earlier in the day?

When are you eating in the evening? Are you giving your body a chance to digest what you've eaten before heading to bed or could late-night snacking or eating be making a difference? Eating too early can also have an impact as heading to bed hungry isn't great either – how can you work this out in your own life?

Are you moving your body at some point in the day and are you getting natural light into your eyes from early on? Working out at the end of the day can suit some people but, for others, it can affect their sleep – does something need to be looked at here?

THE STORIES WE TELL OURSELVES

We love a good story, don't we? Stories are read to us as children until we can read them for ourselves.

Did you know that we also tell ourselves stories? All through the day – and sometimes well into the night – we have a ticker-tape of thoughts running through our heads. Often, these thoughts are things on our to-do list, the things we still have to get done. Or they could be things that have already happened – we might dwell on a conversation, an event or a memory.

But aside from fleeting thoughts, there are thoughts that play on repeat, that begin to shape who we are. These are the stories we tell ourselves about who we are and what we are capable of.

Sadly, many of the things we tell ourselves are negative. In 2005, research published by the National Science Foundation revealed that the average person has about 12,000 to 60,000 thoughts per day. Of those, 95 per cent are exactly the same repetitive thoughts as the day before and about 80 per cent are negative. It's hard to take in really, isn't it? If I asked you to tune in to a recording every day of someone saying bad things about you, you wouldn't want to listen because you'd say it would bring you down, yet you allow thousands of negative thoughts to roll around your mind every single day.

We all do it. Some more consciously than others, but we all tell ourselves we are not good enough, smart enough, doing enough – just not enough. We might tell ourselves that there are things we could never do because we wouldn't have the time, the money, the nerve or the personality. We rarely challenge these stories and are often unaware of the power they hold over us and how they shape the lives we live.

My friend Georgie told herself for years that she wasn't a runner and that she didn't really like being outside because it was too cold. But she challenged this mindset and, one step at a time, became a runner. She now heads up the Team Good Glow running club with her husband Jamie, and they have taken groups to run all over the world. How many people in that group also changed the story they told themselves to lead them there? What would they have missed by staying stuck in the one story?

Another friend, Miheala, spent many years as a beauty therapist listening to people pour their hearts out in the privacy of treatment rooms (myself included), and a spark went off that she would like to be able to do something more with this gift she had to hold space for people to open up. She told herself stories about how she couldn't do that – how would she find the time and the money to train? – but, thankfully, she didn't tell herself those for too long and she recently qualified as a psychotherapist.

We don't start out as the people we would like to be, we become the people we want to be one small step at a time. Turning the dial down on your inner critic and putting the positive in is one of the most crucial steps.

For years, I told myself that I wasn't a morning person. It wasn't just myself telling that story but my family and friends too. As a teen my family's nickname for me was 'Sun Don't Shine in the Morning'. So, I continued to hide myself behind the cornflakes box, barked when questioned and took this character trait with me when I moved out.

Even though I spent years working the breakfast shift, I still told myself that I wasn't a morning person. I would be up, dressed and blow-dried ready for the cameras of *Ireland AM* before 7 a.m., five days a week with a smile on my face and joy in my heart but still didn't think I was a morning person. I didn't have a glam squad to help me get ready when I worked on *The*

Ian Dempsey Breakfast Show, but I would still be primed and ready to go for the 6.15 a.m. meeting – and still considered myself not to be a morning person.

Around 2001, an online course caught my eye called *Wake Up Well*. It involved meditation, breathwork and some movement for forty-five minutes from 6 a.m., so I decided to give it a go. This routine went against the strongly held beliefs I had about what I was capable of. I showed up the first morning bleary-eyed – I was most likely late – but I settled down in front of my phone on my couch and it was the first day of the rest of my life.

It took a while for the positive message to sink in. Most mornings, I would have to drag myself downstairs, grumbling as I went. One particular morning, cacao-drinking was suggested, and I had a disaster involving my blender, hot liquid and a dark-brown explosion up my wall – hardly a zen moment. However, all that aside, I began to notice that after taking time for myself in the morning, I didn't react to my kids as much when they weren't putting their shoes on and we were running late, and the traffic didn't seem to bug me as much. In fact, I was more likely to be singing along to the radio as my energy levels were up. On the days I didn't do this morning routine, I would experience the reverse, reacting to situations and dragging myself through the day like I was pulling through wet cement.

What I began to realise was that a day started slowly, investing in myself, was ultimately a better day. It's a habit that I've kept with me. It's not always forty-five minutes – and I often lack the finesse of the three practitioners who led us through each of the disciplines of mindfulness, breathwork and movement on that course – but most days, for at least ten minutes before everyone else gets up, I sit, with my candle and my cup, and I take a moment, just for me.

If I feel I need a bit more sleep for whatever reason, that's fine, I go with it. And sometimes I just sit and catch up on WhatsApps and have a social-media flick – though that is far less restorative than the meditation or breathwork. The important part is that it is *my time* and it enables me to start the day in a low gear and give to myself before I give to others. It's so simple but so powerful.

Those two little words – *my time* – can have such an impact on your life. In an online course I once hosted, a participant said that the mornings just weren't for her in terms of relaxation. She couldn't help but look around her at what needed to be done that day and was simply raring to get stuck into it. So, instead, she chose the evening time when her kids had gone to bed and the day was done. She would sit with a cup of tea and nothing else, no agenda. But those few minutes were hers. She had also shared that she felt a little stuck in her job and was unsure of what to do next, and while there was no pressure on her to spend this time with her cuppa figuring it all out and devising a plan to resolve these issues, the stillness brought her all kinds of insights – she needed to slow down to hear them.

Within the constant babble we have going on about what we could or should be doing, it's good to just sit and be gentle with yourself, a moment of peace within the noise.

Did I have a *me time* morning when I had babies feeding through the night? No. Did I light a candle when the alarm went off at 4 a.m. for *Ireland AM*? No, I didn't. There will be chapters and seasons in your life where you will just have to go with the flow. But I also have a very different mindset now to when I was on breakfast television or was a new mum, and if I was to have that time again, I would find different points in my day to give myself those ten or fifteen minutes. I know it would have helped me during such busy times in my life.

I would never have discovered this had I stuck with the old narrative. Instead, I chose to rewrite my own story. I went from someone who constantly hit the snooze button, drove my parents crazy, was eternally late for college lectures and then my nine-to-five job, to someone who 'became' a morning person. I've done sunrise hikes, swims and even hosted a breathwork session on the beach at 6 a.m. There's such a special feeling at that time of the morning, the feeling that anything is possible and it is all just beginning. To watch the sun come up is truly magical and I missed so many sunrises because of the story I told myself about who I was.

We can't rewrite history, but we can reprogramme the stories we tell ourselves. We can take steps towards change that can take us to places we didn't think were possible. What story are you telling yourself about yourself? Are you going to let that be just the way it is or are you going to step into a new chapter?

WELL? OVER TO YOU ...

What's your story?

What are some of the stories you have told yourself about the type of person you are – or aren't? What adjectives would you use to describe yourself?

What would you say are your best qualities?

What would you say are your worst qualities?

How would a best friend describe you?

Think of some things that you would love to do but you're not sure you could. Marathon? Successful relationship? Run your own business? Travel the world? Go on a retreat solo? Take up a new hobby?

If you think you can't do any of them, what's stopping you?

When was the last time you surprised yourself and did something you thought you couldn't?

When was the last time you challenged yourself?

What would really put you out of your comfort zone?

Could you say 'no' to something you always say 'yes' to?

NEGATIVITY BIAS

Our brains are amazing protection devices designed to keep us safe, therefore they will always predict the worse-case scenario in any situation. The default is also to conserve energy, so when you think about heading out for a walk or a run, you'll feel that pull to the couch. I used to drive myself demented when I went to evening workout classes. All day, I would battle in my head about going, telling myself I was tired or busy or whatever other excuse I'd pull in. This would rage in my head right up to me arriving at the gym, where I would complete the class and leave elated. What a way to waste time and energy.

I found the same thing happening with sea swimming. I was never one to get into the sea – for years I'd go to places like Spain and Portugal and wouldn't get in – but when the pandemic hit, my diary cleared and my anxiety went through the roof, so I got a dry robe and headed to the coast. I grew up in the most picturesque seaside village but it took a bat in Wuhan to get me into the waves. I would meet my friends at sunrise, get in the freezing sea and then sit with a flask of something warm afterwards, catching up and feeling invincible. I remember one time deciding that I wouldn't get in, that I'd rather just chat to the beautiful community that really made the sea experience, but when I went back to my car that day, my heart was full from the gorgeous souls but I wasn't buzzing. You get the buzz when you get in.

So why, with all that information and experience, do I arrive to the sea with a sense of dread about getting in? Again, my inner dialogue is ping-ponging around my head about being too tired, the water being too cold – too much of whatever you're having yourself. I gingerly creep towards the water and edge my way in – I'm always last to fully submerge. And then I acclimatise – I love it and I don't want to get out again. Last in, last out, flipping around like a mermaid with a full head dunk every time for the reset. Buzzing. Why don't I remember that? I do, of course, but the overriding sense is one of dread.

It's because of our negativity bias. Our brain's protection system, keeping us safe from harm. If we didn't have it, Lord knows what we'd be getting up to. We are pretty wild as humans already, with our bungie-jumping and cliff-diving, but without the brain's protectiveness, we'd be flinging ourselves off the top of buildings rather than taking the lift or stairs – we need the bit of caution.

But be aware of its presence. Let it hold you back from endangering yourself, but don't let it hold you back from what you need. Hear it, acknowledge it but know that you can override it for the greater good. It comes back to balance, that sweet spot of inner knowing – when to listen and when to ignore. There are times when you do need to rest on the couch and have an early night instead of a run, but that's not what you need every night, is it?

Pushing ourselves can be healthy when it's kept in balance. Getting comfortable with the uncomfortable is where the growth and learning is. I used to think that our comfort zone was, as the name suggests, comfy, in the positive sense of the word, but actually our comfort zone can be negative, a space where we remain stuck because it's familiar. What is familiar to us is safe, but it may not be serving us in the long term. Expect resistance to change – we spoke already about walking a new path and the extra effort that's required, it's going to feel rough at the beginning until you adapt and evolve.

Imposter syndrome

Imposter syndrome is doubting your abilities and fearing others will discover this self-perceived inadequacy. I'm glad it's something we've started to talk about more as it helps us realise that everybody experiences it. We are all amateurs until we get some air miles under our belt, it's part of the process of learning something new.

When I was learning how to drive, I was shocked at how complicated it was – so much more complicated than a bumper car! I literally thought that it would be hit a button to start up and then accelerate or brake was all you needed. I did hope I wouldn't bump into other cars on the roads, of course, but I did not think there would be a clutch and 'biting point' to get my head around, as well as gears to go up and down – and that was before I even began with the rules of the road. I thought that I would never get to a comfortable stage with driving, that I would never be able to chat to a passenger in the car or listen to music. And then, obviously, the more I did it, the better I became, and this built my confidence. It's the same with most experiences – everyone feels imposter syndrome the first few times they do something, when it is all new. So, when you feel it, notice it, acknowledge it, but don't let it determine whether or not you continue with something.

When training to teach breathwork recently (more on this later), so many of the brilliant people I learnt alongside were doubting their ability to use their new-found skills to teach a class. I understand that anything new is daunting, particularly standing up in front of a group, but I shared with some of them that even though that is very much part of my job, I still felt fearful holding my first session. Fear of the unknown, fear of stepping out of our comfort zone is just part of the process. It's shouldn't be the decider as to whether or not you continue.

Fake it until you make it; experience quashes fear and you only gain experience by taking it one step at a time. Even if you find you don't like something or it's just not for you, at least you tried. Often, it's the things we didn't do that we regret more than the things we did. I never want to wonder 'what if', I want to give everything I can a go.

Like writing this book, for example. Even though it was something I had wanted to do for a long time and I have a message that I am passionate about, there were many times when I had the inner voice asking, *Who do you think you are, writing a book?* But it's an opportunity that came my way, so I'm going to grab it. How would I feel if I'd turned it down because I was worried about what others would think or that I wasn't good enough? Sometimes, you have to just take a leap and go for it.

My favourite quotation comes from Marianne Williamson's 1992 book *A Return to Love*.

> *Our deepest fear is not that we are inadequate. Our deepest fear is that we are powerful beyond measure. It is our light, not our darkness that most frightens us. We ask ourselves, 'Who am I to be brilliant, gorgeous, talented, fabulous?' Actually, who are you not to be?*

How true is that? One of my most motivating factors that I return to again and again is that we only get one precious life.

To be content with what we have is a beautiful way to live, but if there is something you want, something you dream for yourself, then why not give it a go? Don't count yourself out of anything, everyone is incapable until they are capable.

And when you do put yourself out there or give something new a go, celebrate yourself. It's huge, whatever the outcome. You took a chance on yourself.

Mel Robbins, bestselling author, podcaster and expert on behaviour change, often speaks on her podcast about feeling stuck. When we are tired, we sleep, when we're thirsty, we drink, when we're hungry, we eat – and when we feel stuck, it is because we are not growing. Our lives have too much of the same. To learn and to try something new is to grow.

The learning zone

The Learning Zone Model was developed by German educator and adventurer Tom Senninger in 2000. The model outlines that in order to learn successfully – to enter the learning zone – we must be challenged to push beyond our comfort zone. The comfort zone covers the routines you currently have and know. However, if we push too far, we enter the alarm zone and can become overwhelmed or stressed, and are more likely to give up. The sweet spot is the learning zone, where you experiment, stretch your abilities and develop new skills.

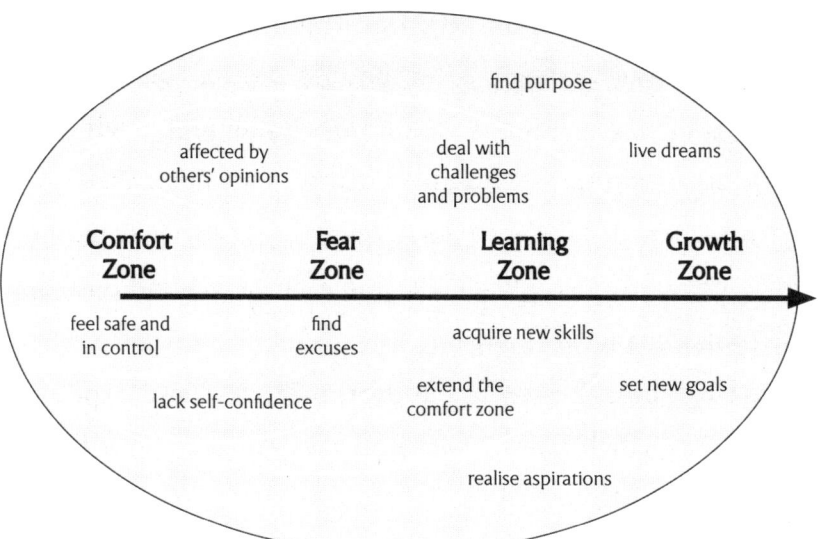

Figure 2: The learning zone model

Commit to pushing yourself to try new things, become comfortable in the learning zone rather than stressing yourself out. Being in what is known as the 'growth mindset' can add an exciting energy to your life.

The message that we have the ability to create the life we want to lead from the inside out can be overwhelming, but it can also be empowering. Change requires effort and determination but the journey can be paved with learning and joy. Often, I have set out to achieve something – learn a new skill, get a new job – and while things haven't gone exactly as I'd imagined they would, so many other doors have opened along the way. I have made new connections and learnt so much about myself.

Our mindset is a powerful force on any wellness journey. By setting your starting point to one of self-love and self-compassion, you can build a solid foundation and, from there, embrace learning and change.

There may be parts of our outer world that we cannot change, but we can change our inner world – how we think, the decisions we make, the actions we take and how we show up for ourselves.

Mindset tools

Affirmations

Affirmations can be a great way to get the more positive thought loops going in your head and dial down the inner critic – give them a go for two to four weeks and see if you notice a difference.

Saying affirmations aloud can feel uncomfortable and even a bit cringey sometimes; I have felt it myself. But remember – you have negative affirmations rolling around in your head all the time, so replacing them is worth a go. Putting the positive in, especially first thing in the morning or at the start of your day, can set a stronger mindset – where focus goes, energy flows. So are you putting your energy into the positive or the negative?

> I have a free audio track at www.wouldyoubewell.ie

I am doing the best that I can.

I am powerful beyond measure.

I love and accept myself.

I deserve all the good things in my life.

I have the courage to take on life's challenges.

I am worthy of love and happiness.

I am a powerful force.

I am the creator of my own reality.

I choose to focus on the good in my life.

I am open to new opportunities.

I am worthy of rest and self-care.

I am enough.

All is well.

I am grateful for every day.

Vision board

If you're a more visual person, a vision board can be a great way to set your intentions for the year ahead (or however long you're comfortable with) and to give you clarity on what you want. Cutting out pictures and words or phrases and sticking them onto a piece of paper or card can not only enable you to feel the freedom you had as a child to express yourself through art, but can also conjure up feelings of what you want to achieve. Dream big – this is just for you, have fun with it.

Journalling

Journalling is basically getting thoughts out of your head and onto paper. I struggle with this one and it doesn't feature in my everyday. This is the message I really want to get into this book: you don't have to do every wellness endeavour in order to be well, you can try them out and see what works for you.

Julia Cameron's book *The Artist's Way* is a twelve-week programme designed to unlock creativity and overcome creative blocks. One of the steps is 'Morning Pages', which suggests taking a pen and paper first thing in the morning and free-writing for three pages, whatever comes to mind, just writing. This is the thing about journalling: we imagine it all has to make sense like a to-do list or a diary entry but it doesn't at all – forget grammar and punctuation rules, no one will be reading this let alone correcting it, this is just for you. Try it for a month and see how you go, you never know where it might lead.

Gratitude

When we express or receive gratitude, our brains release dopamine and serotonin, which enhances feelings of calm, happiness, focus, motivation and contentment. Practising gratitude on an ongoing basis can help strengthen these neural pathways.

Before going to bed, write down three things you are grateful for from the day. They can be big or small – a hug from your child, a parking spot close to the supermarket, a sunny day, your plant grew a flower. Think of those three things as you close out your day. Over time, your brain will begin seeking out items for the list.

If you have children, this is a great habit to give them as you say goodnight – it's good for us to be on the lookout for all the good in our lives.

Mindfulness and meditation

These two words are like a double-edged sword. On the one hand, they are scientifically proven methods entrenched in age-old wisdom that can really support you in life, but, on the other hand, they can strike fear into the hearts of many, who think:

1. How the hell do I do it?
2. Where am I supposed to fit them in?

The major issue is the hype, and the stereotype of a monk in a temple sitting for hours on end contemplating life. While, yes, we can all recognise this is a very beautiful and no doubt illuminating way to live your life, when you have kids and/or a career and the weight of the world on your shoulders with modern living, the chance would be a fine thing. The irony is that the more you have going on in life, the more mindfulness and meditation can help support you.

Let's break them down by definition.

mindfulness

noun

1. the quality or state of being conscious or aware of something.
2. a mental state achieved by focusing one's awareness on the present moment, while calmly acknowledging and accepting one's feelings, thoughts and bodily sensations; used as a therapeutic technique.

meditate

verb

focus one's mind for a period of time, in silence or with the aid of chanting, for religious or spiritual purposes or as a method of relaxation.

You may have noticed that both definitions allude to focusing on the here and the now. Our minds will have us perpetually in the past or the future, so we will be thinking of our to-do list or worrying about what might or might not happen, or we might be dwelling on what has already happened. While some forward planning and some reflection on what has already occurred can no doubt be helpful, when it is constant, it can wear us down. Being present and in the moment means we are more rooted and grounded in our life.

I have struggled with this and still often go off-track. I want to put my hand up and say the book *The Power of Now* by world-renowned author and speaker Eckhart Tolle sat unread on my bookshelf for years. The title screamed *NOW* and yet I still put it on the long finger. The present moment can elude us all!

Let's take the monk-style pressure off – you don't have to be mindful or meditate for hours on end. The good news is that seconds or minutes is good enough.

Can we return to Eckhart Tolle for a moment? His story is pretty incredible and can give a level of understanding to mindfulness and meditation. His books have sold millions of copies worldwide and he counts Oprah and Deepak Chopra among his fans, but his life was very different when, at twenty-nine, he experienced depression and suicidal thoughts. It was during this time that a thought came into his head, *I cannot live with myself any longer.* In this moment, he realised that there were two Eckharts described in that sentence – the 'I' and 'myself' – and it not only made him step back and observe his thoughts but he also began to question which was the more important one to be listening to? Which one was telling the truth? Which one was his true self and which one was the listener? It made him realise that he had control over his thoughts.

Thus began a massive journey of healing that he went on to share with the world and it is the essence of mindfulness and meditation – coming into the present moment, becoming aware of your thoughts, stepping back and observing them and beginning to question whether they are helpful or true.

To do this, you need to bring yourself into the present moment, you need to become aware – of your surroundings and of your thoughts. This is where mindfulness and meditation come in.

Let's start with meditation – sitting or lying quietly, becoming still and taking a moment to see what bubbles up. One of the biggest misconceptions about meditating is that you have to clear your mind of all thoughts, but that's like asking your veins to stop pumping blood – clearing your mind of thoughts is equally impossible. What you want to do is try to slow down your thoughts, to become aware of them rather than simply allowing them to run wild and free in your head. This will be different for everyone, particularly those with neurodivergence, but, essentially, take a moment, become still – however that looks for you – take a deep breath and listen. Random thoughts will fly in about your hairdresser, what to have for dinner, what you said last night ... allow the thoughts to come but don't follow them – park them and come back to the present moment.

Over time, you will grow stronger and begin to settle more easily, but bringing yourself back to the present moment is where the power is – you are meditating when you do that.

This is where mindfulness comes in – being mindful in the present moment. The body and the breath is always present; the mind is often in the past or future, so bring it back to feeling your body against the chair or the bed, your feet on the ground, your breath. The moment you catch yourself thinking about what to cook with that chicken breast later and you bring yourself back – you've won, you're mindful, that's the skill. The more you do it, like any muscle you flex, the stronger you become at it.

The science of mindfulness shows it can alter brain structure and function, improving emotional regulation and resilience. Research indicates that mindfulness practices decrease activity in the amygdala (the brain's fear centre) while increasing activity in the prefrontal cortex and hippocampus, which are associated with emotional control and self-awareness (Keng, Smoski & Robins, 2011).

You don't have to sit on a fancy cushion or in a temple, you can bring mindfulness into your everyday life.

- When you're driving the car – catch your thoughts drifting off and come back to the present moment and take a deep breath (eyes open).
- When you're in the shower, really *be* in the shower – feel the water on your head and your skin, listen to its sound and take a deep breath.
- When you're washing up at the sink – really *be there* – feel the water on your hands, look at each dish and take a deep breath.
- When you're brushing your teeth or lifting weights in the gym – allow yourself time to be fully present.
- I often find cooking can be mindful and meditative as it is all I am focused on, likewise baking. When I'm in the gym I am often so immersed in the rep counts that I've stopped thinking about anything else.
- Breathwork – three deep breaths – can bring you into the present moment. (More of this to follow.)

Whatever you do in life, aim to be as present as possible, particularly with your people, but remember: go gentle and start by weaving these mindful and meditative moments into your day.

Little micro-moments like this can make a massive difference – they build up and come together, stopping you from sleep-walking through your life with your thoughts running riot.

There are so many distractions in modern life that it's more pertinent than ever that we do our best to bring ourselves back to be in the moment. I can't tell you how many times I've picked up my phone to do one task and found myself sucked into another, then mindlessly scrolling, only to forget the reason I picked it up in the first place – how often is this energy showing up in other areas of our lives? Missing what's important and getting stuff done.

Our smartphones and connectivity have brought so much to our lives but what have they taken away? One thing for sure is the ability to be truly present for the people in our lives and for ourselves.

I have some tips for making your beloved smartphone a little less distracting.

- **Turn off notifications:** We don't need to be constantly alerted about every news and social-media update – you decide when you go in. And while doom-scrolling is almost par for the course these days, again, you decide when you get sucked in. The optimum is that you plan your scrolling time and regardless of how long you spend, enjoy it – as opposed to allowing it to drag you in over and over again, leaving you exhausted and feeling guilty.
- **Keep it on silent:** This will be different for everyone depending on the responsibilities in your life, but, if you can, I say switch it to silent! Mine went to silent when I had my

first baby fourteen years ago and it's rarely been on ring since. I turn it on if I'm expecting an important call but 99 per cent of the time, it's on silent and I can count on one hand the number of times I've missed an important call. And guess what – they can call back and so can you!

- **Use your phone for good**: Relaxing music, meditation apps, podcasts, audiobooks … there is a lot of good stuff so we don't need to demonise our phones. I personally keep mine out of my room at night and it's been a game-changer. But, again, this depends on your life situation and also your ability to be disciplined – if you can have it in your room and it's not keeping you from your rest or sleep, particularly if using it for the good stuff, then what's the harm? It comes back to being mindful of how you are using your phone – are you in control of your usage or is it in control of you?

Try and ensure that your phone is not the first thing you look at in the morning and the last thing you look at at night. Tricky, I know, but even having a fifteen-minute buffer, longer if possible – where you read, listen to music, sit with your morning cuppa, get outside – will make all the difference before you plug yourself back into the mainframe!

Voice-command technology means we often don't need to pick up our phones to play music or an audiobook or to stop our alarm. I also got myself an alarm clock, which eradicated that need, but as I said, you do you.

And you do you when it comes to mindfulness and meditation. Whether you spend ten minutes listening to a guided meditation or one minute becoming aware of your thoughts – you can stop on your walk and just take in your surroundings or simply take a deep breath in the car – bringing yourself into the present moment in a way that works for you is a wellness endeavour worth paying attention to. There are lots of free apps and guided meditations on YouTube – though you can also just sit and breathe.

- **Deepak Chopra App:** I love when a series is released as it's a targeted challenge to show up for the forty days – they are always excellent.
- **Insight Timer:** Sara Blondin and her dreamy voice and way with words is my top listen, but there are loads you can pick according to the time you have.

I have guided meditations, visualisation, breathwork and sleep audios on my website – www.wouldyoubewell.ie – others well worth checking out are:
- **Fiona Brennan:** thepositivehabit.com
- **Miriam and Gerry Hussey:** soulspace.ie
- **Georgie Crawford:** thegoodglow.ie
- **Dermot Whelan:** dermotwhelan.com
- **Roxie Nafousi:** roxienafousi.com

WELL? OVER TO YOU ...

Answer the following questions without judgement – not many people are immune to the pull of the smartphone.

How do you feel about your smartphone usage? (Use a scale of 1 to 10 where 1 is 'not great at all' and 10 is 'great'.)

Do you feel you are in control of your screen time or is it in control of you?

Do you find yourself mindlessly scrolling instead of doing things you want to do?

What are you not finding time for in life that you'd like to do more of?

How do you feel when you come off your phone? (Use a scale of 1 to 10 where 1 is 'not great at all' and 10 is 'great')

What are the feelings your phone usage brings up?

What is your average daily screen time?

How much of that is related to things you need to do, for example life admin, work, keeping in touch, etc?

How much time would you like to give to scrolling?

Do you allow yourself time to truly immerse yourself and enjoy your time on your phone?

What changes could you make to bring more control and more enjoyment to your phone use?

DOING THE WORK

We don't want to do the work, do we? Not really. I mean, we are already doing so much work – from our actual jobs to minding the people in our lives. We're all trying to eat well, work out, rest, meditate, stretch, let our hair down, be caring, go with the flow – it's exhausting! We want to be part of our community, part of something bigger, keep up with world events and to make a difference. It's a lot.

Unfortunately, that's not all. There is perhaps even more important work to be done, and that's the work on ourselves. This consists of self-enquiry, shining a light within so we can figure out why we feel the way we feel and why we do what we do.

It is by no means easy. For some, it will be deeply traumatic and may require the assistance of a professional to work through it all. In fact, I think therapy should be far more accessible – we are all faced with challenges in life, and to be supported through those times as the norm would make the world a better place.

Psychologists will often refer to 'big T' and 'little t' trauma. 'Big T' traumas are things such as war, abuse, violence and neglect. 'Little t' traumas are break-ups, separation, financial stress, family issues, moving house, changing career, death – the parts of life that are not uncommon but that are still difficult to navigate. Having a psychotherapist to speak honestly and openly with, who is trauma-informed and able to help you through, is something that everybody should be able to do. Thankfully, therapy is becoming more common and no longer a practice we scoff at or view as something only Americans do. We now, more commonly, understand that talking about our feelings is a very important part of how we show up in the world. If you don't know how you feel, then you can't ask for what you need.

There will be things from your past that have shaped you – some good but also others that can hold you back and keep you stuck. You can be shaped by your family of origin – in our childhood, we're like sponges, we soak up everything and it determines so much about how we understand communication and relationships.

You will often see the same mannerisms, sense of humour and even opinions filter down through families. From religion to football teams and even what we believe we are capable of. It fascinates me how children of doctors often go on to be doctors. Part of this is due to them having the means to fund an education but it's also down to a child growing up and watching this career path day in and day out.

I worked with a woman who told me about her struggle with a sense of abandonment. It was something that kept showing up in her life, in particular her relationships, and when she spent some time reflecting on it, she traced it back in part to being left with a childminder when she was young and the feeling she had as her mum drove away. There were no issues with the childminder, she was very well cared for and she can logically understand that her mother had to work and is happy and proud of that fact, but logic doesn't erase that original feeling. Recognising where this is coming from is one of the first steps to freedom from it.

Anthony de Mello was an Indian priest and psychotherapist who became well known for his public speaking and bestselling books on spirituality. He has a fantastic quotation in his book *Awareness* (2000): 'What we aren't aware of controls us and what we are aware of we control.'

So, if I take the example above: rather than pushing that discomfort away – ridiculing herself for a ridiculous overreaction to being left with a childminder when she was perfectly safe – but instead making peace with and honouring the feelings this woman had as a little girl is a very powerful release. The next time it shows up in a romantic relationship or friendship, there is more of an opportunity for her to catch the thought and recognise its origins, enabling her to make sense of her reactions and let them go.

I had to do this work myself. I'm someone who didn't think I had anything that needed major exploration, there was no major trauma in my life – in fact, I was very lucky, loved and privileged. Something I knew had been a stress in my life, but which I had also made sense of and peace with, was the fact that I fought with my parents throughout my teenage years. This is pretty standard but it resulted in me moving out of my family home aged eighteen.

I was born to my loving parents after they had struggled with fertility for five years and then, after me, they had to wait another five years before they had 'Irish twins', my brother and sister born in quick succession. I adore my siblings and we are an extremely close family, but the age gap between us caused some issues. It was tricky to have two small kids at the bath-and-bedtime stage with another seeking independence and more time with her peers, and so we fought.

I moved out when I was in my second year at drama college. My parents paid my rent for the first year and when I left college, I started working full-time in an office and was studying marketing at night and paid my own way. Moving out was the making of my relationship with my parents; I had the independence that I craved, so that stress was gone. I also knew I could call on them if I ever needed anything and there were times when I was sick or heartbroken when I did just that, as well as the regular visits for Mum's dinner. Like I said, we are a very Brady Bunch-type of family, lots of hugs, lots of laughter and lots of singing! Far from estranged, we were always – and still are – very close; I never lived very far away and we were often together. My dad died in 2020, and, as I write this book, I am back living with my mum, with my own family in tow and a plan to build a house next door, so all is very well. My mum is and has always been an incredible support to me. And my kids adore her, everyone does.

However, there were scars from those difficult teenage years that I had to eventually face up to. The fighting hurt me. Yes, I had my obnoxious teenage part to play in it, but I often felt misunderstood, unsupported and that I wasn't being listened to. I often felt like nothing I did was right. We went to family counselling at one point; I can't remember much about the sessions themselves, but I do remember there were tears, and I do remember wishing that the counsellor would suggest that we work on the relationship, that we make some one-on-one time – a trip to the cinema with my dad, a walk or dinner just with my mum – but he never did. In fact, in what would be our final counselling session, he suggested that it would be best if I moved out. Irreconcilable differences, I suppose.

My dad was the most gorgeous man, friendly and loved by all, me included, but he could be strict. He was a lot less strict than his parents had been on him – he grew up in an era when the cane was a common part of discipline at home and in the classroom. We did not have the cane. He would talk to us and lay down the ground rules and you didn't go against what he said.

He was adamant that I should move out, as he felt it would be best for everyone. He gave me the newspaper to find myself somewhere – I still remember the sting of that. I also remember my younger brother and sister being caught up in the arguments, innocent bystanders listening to the shouting. And, while it wasn't verbalised, I felt they must, on some level, have been relieved to see me go because it meant the tension in the house was reduced.

In more recent years, my sister, who is one of my best friends in the world, said to me that it must have hurt to go, and I felt something inside me shift. That acknowledgement meant everything. It also made me realise that while I hadn't dwelled on the experience, there were parts that I had always carried with me.

It was showing up in my work. I chose an industry that requires a fairly thick skin, as rejection is as regular as the hustle required to succeed. I had plenty of moxie and a have-a-go attitude – I believed in myself – but when things didn't go as I thought they might with some presenting gigs, I would often slope off for far too long rather than take a moment, dust myself off and try again.

Rejection is redirection, after all. And here I was living my best life. When I had moved out of home, I flew. I had fun, embraced life and still had the full support of my family every step of the way, but I had to concede that being asked to leave home was the ultimate rejection from my primary caregivers – that's how it had felt in the moment. Years later, my dad took me out for dinner – we met for concerts and dinner regularly – and he asked me how I felt about it all. Did I feel they had let me down in any way? I told him they hadn't, genuinely. I said it was the making of me, which it was in many ways. I knew they did what they truly felt was best. I still stand by that, but this rejection was showing up not just in my work life but in romantic relationships too, where I was co-dependent and constantly seeking validation.

I didn't want to shine a light back into my past. I didn't want to go over it all again because what was the point? We were all fine. People are living in war-torn countries, experiencing untold abuse and here was little old me having a moan because I was told to move out when I was eighteen, like millions of people do the world over heading off to college or to work.

But, like a football you try to push down under the water, this feeling will keep popping back up to the surface unless you let it float free.

So that's what I did: I faced it. I sat with it and I talked to a therapist. I didn't feel the need to go and discuss it all with my family, this was just my perspective, my feelings, and I worked through them. Do I love rejection now? Am I perfect in all my relationships now? Of course not, but I now recognise when a thought comes into my head that is linked to that time.

I had started a loop that I wasn't good enough. I wasn't good enough to live in my family home. When I didn't get a gig, it was like another stamp of confirmation that I wasn't good enough. When a romantic relationship broke down, it was because I wasn't good enough. It's a negative energy to be in and it kept me stuck. Now, if that thought pattern crops up, I think, *There's that old pattern again*. I recognise it, and that recognition is a hug of sorts. I don't fight it, I accept it – it doesn't hold power anymore.

I have had many supports outside of and alongside therapy, including life coaches and reiki healers. It's important that you keep in mind what each is qualified to deal with but to have someone objective in your life that you trust and can lean on, to sit with and have them hold space for you to share what's going on in life, can be transformative. When you have that lightbulb moment of realisation you can't unsee it and it begins to inform your decisions and actions in a more positive way. You understand yourself better.

I had a friend whose parents separated – her mother remarried and had more children. My pal adored her siblings and cherished her second family life but because she was so much older, she helped a lot with the younger children. This caring role became a source of validation for her and she constantly found herself in the caregiver role, often putting the needs of others ahead of her own. It wasn't something she was bitter about, but it was a pattern that had started in childhood and went on to shape her adulthood. When she made the connection, it didn't mean she never helped another soul, but it did mean that she noticed when her tendency towards people-pleasing was taking priority over her own self-care. She became stronger in her own foundation and with her own energy and boundaries, so that now when she is helping others out it isn't draining her but can light her up and make her feel good.

That's the work. It is ever-evolving and ever-unfolding but the more you get to know yourself and why you do what you do, the more you can show up for yourself and ask for what you need. Ignorance isn't bliss as it turns out; it's better to be aware and get the skeletons out of the closet so you use that space to hang things that serve you better instead.

Finding the therapist who is right for you

1. **Consult your GP**

    Your doctor can provide a referral to a therapist or suggest suitable services.

    Check if you qualify for free counselling through the National Counselling Service (NCS) if you have a medical card or have experienced childhood abuse.

2. **Check professional organisations online to find therapists in your local area and find out what services they offer**

    Search the Psychological Society of Ireland's online directory for psychologists.

    Check the Irish Association for Counselling and Psychotherapy website for accredited therapists.

    There are a many different types of therapy, including:
    - *Psychodynamic*: Delving into the unconscious and our past and bringing it into the conscious.
    - *Trauma therapy and eye movement desensitisation and reprocessing (EMDR)*: Deals very effectively with traumas that are 'stuck'.
    - *Gestalt therapy*: Focuses very much on the client experience in the present moment.
    - *Cognitive behavioural therapy (CBT)*: Addresses mal-adaptive thoughts, behaviour patterns and core beliefs that are not always supportive or helpful.

3. **It's important that you feel comfortable with your therapist**

    Yes, there may be uncomfortable moments and it may be challenging to open up or get used to the process but you should get an instinct early on about whether you can build a trusting relationship.

    If you don't feel comfortable with a therapist, it's okay to try someone else. Likewise, if after a time you feel you are no longer growing from the experience, it's okay to move to another therapist or practice. You may also increase and decrease the amount of time you spend in therapy at various times in your life.

4. **Consider cost and location**

    Explore if your health insurance covers therapy, or if you can access lower-cost options. Your workplace may also have access to a therapist through the Employee Assistance Programme (EAP). If you can afford therapy, consider it as an investment in yourself. There should be no stigma in seeking the support you need.

5. **Read reviews and ask for recommendations**

    See what others say about therapists and consider asking friends, family or colleagues for recommendations.

6. **Consider online and telephone therapy**

    If you have difficulty accessing in-person therapy meet a therapist online or over the phone.

SHOW UP FOR YOURSELF

We've looked at our thoughts and how they influence our behaviours and habits, as well as the importance of putting the positive in there. How does that then show up in our everyday actions and how should we handle a setback?

Sometimes, I'll find myself slipping back to some sort of body-image negativity or self-doubt and I just stop it in its tracks, reminding myself that I don't do that anymore. We also need to have self-compassion, to give ourselves a break and to recognise that we are doing the best we can. Dr Kristin Neff, Associate Professor of Educational Psychology at the University of Texas, has researched the area of self-compassion since the early 2000s and has published several papers and books on the topic. She found that the practice of self-compassion can reduce perceived stress by helping individuals to self-regulate the so-called 'negative' emotions that can follow when outcomes or situations arise that we weren't expecting. That is not to say that traumatic events are to be underestimated but, for everyday issues and struggles that can arise, their impact can be lessened when we stop giving ourselves such a hard time.

Failure is a natural part of learning and life. I am such a fan of the writer and podcaster Elizabeth Day, whose career has gone to stratospheric heights since the launch of her brilliant podcast *How to Fail*. Elizabeth found herself single in her late thirties when her marriage ended. Throughout it, they had tried to have a child and had gone through several rounds of IVF. She felt adrift and like a failure at thirty-nine.

She became fascinated with the subject of failure – why we rarely talk about it and why we fear it so much. Her podcast asks people of note to discuss three perceived failures in their lives and what it has taught them, if anything. It's so interesting to hear that no matter how successful we think someone is, no journey is without failure. The definition needs a rebrand as it's often viewed as the end, when it really is just part of the process and often a new beginning. If you're failing, you are trying and you are learning about yourself and the world. It shouldn't hold the fear that it does.

Consider the analogy of a baby learning to go from crawling to walking. They wobble, they fall over, but they smile and they try again. We don't discourage them, and we don't start thinking that they will never walk. We should give ourselves the same level of support, celebrating every small step and comforting and encouraging ourselves during every wobble.

When it comes to dropping a ball – forgetting a birthday, losing your keys – this is normal, we are human. It's literally impossible to be all things to everyone, so go easy on yourself, take the ball-drop as a moment to reassess everything you are juggling and whether you might need more support or to let something go. Under no circumstance are you to spiral into a state of self-loathing because you didn't find the time to papier-mâché a Hogwarts owl for your kid's World Book Day costume.

Change the record from the one where you put yourself down all the time, to the one where you big yourself up or at the very least recognise that you're doing your best. Good enough is good enough. No success journey is linear, there are ups and downs for all of us.

Take action

There is another part of the process. You have to start showing up for yourself, not just with your words but with your actions. So, if you say you are going to do something, you need to just get on with it. Keep in mind everything that I have said about self-compassion and positive self-talk but if you make a promise to yourself to start taking better care of yourself, you have to make it happen.

So, going for the walk, making time for breakfast, trying a new recipe, calling a friend, doing a wardrobe clear-out – when you hear the little whispers about what would make life a little better, then, as the global corporation says, 'just do it'. It's so much better all round when you do the things you say you are going to do. Of course, life commitments can get in the way but you need to find a way through. I'm on your side, I get it, but I know the dirge of the procrastination loop. If you keep saying you'll do something and then do nothing, it starts to drag you down.

This is why it is so important to start small. There is no need to change every facet of your life on a Monday morning. Instead, focus on what you're adding in rather than what you are taking away, and then every time you do the thing you said you were going to, celebrate and be proud. It is not easy to change your habits. And when it's something that brings you joy and makes you feel good or better than you did before – why would you stop?

The psychology of motivation teaches us that small is best. I told you earlier about enlisting the help of coach and author Andy Ramage for my 'what is health and wellness?' challenge. Andy knows a thing or two about motivation. After following a gut feeling that life for him would be better without alcohol, he gave it up and co-founded the movement 'One Year No Beer' to give others the framework to explore their relationship with booze. He found that when he removed it, his life began to flourish – he was sleeping better and so started getting up at 5 a.m. to work out before his corporate-finance job. He started feeling better, so he started eating better and began to get in better shape than he had been for years. His energy levels were better, as were his relationships as he found himself more present with his wife and daughters.

That 5 a.m. start also allowed time to write two books, to study and to qualify in coaching psychology and positive psychology. Andy has now changed his career to coaching and training coaches and, whenever I see him online or in person, he is happier and more fulfilled than the previous time. I saw him post recently that he was heading to walk the Camino on his own, to take time out from social media and do something he'd always wanted to do; he was showing up for himself and making it happen.

His book *Let's Do This: How to Use Motivational Psychology to Change Your Habits for Life* is packed with research and insight, but what I found the most useful was what he told me about how we should start small to really make change. He gave the example of wanting to start meditating. So, usually we say we will do ten minutes every day or we might even go the whole hog and swear we will sit cross-legged for an hour before the sun comes up – either way, he says that's too much. We have to give our minds something we are sure we can achieve, so the first step is to choose how you are going to meditate – are you going to listen to music or perhaps use an app? Say you choose the latter, you download the app. Then for the first couple of weeks at least, every morning, you just have to go to your phone and press the app. That's it. You don't meditate at all! Only after the couple of weeks of just going to the app first thing do you even contemplate actually meditating and, even then it's only for a minute. Your mind is only going to allow you to take the steps you can manage.

Yes, you can still set yourself a large goal like running a marathon or changing your job or moving country, but then you are going to have to break it down into bite-sized chunks. Start with a walk or light jog, find your old CV and update it, google the best place to live right now – the first steps are small, but they all lead to the goal or a journey one way or another.

Adopting the small-steps mindset means you are more likely to celebrate the small wins and it will be a more positive experience regardless of the outcome.

WELL? OVER TO YOU ...

Pick one new habit you would like to take up – jogging, knitting, meditating, listening to podcasts ... whatever it is – let's break it down into smaller steps.

First, let's name what it is you want to do.

What do you need to make it happen? Equipment, for example. (No need to go nuts buying new stuff but if it's meditating you will need to download an app, hunt out your headphones – chances are we have everything we need already.)

How much time per week can you give this? Remember to start small and build up from there.

When will you do this? When will you start and what day/days suit you best?

Where will you do this? What area of the house will you use to meditate, where will you listen to the podcast? What will the route be for your walk or jog?

The reality of every lifestyle change is that there are starts and stops, you might take two steps forward and then fall back – but this isn't failure, it's just the way life goes. There can be all kinds of bumps along the way, but recalibrate and keep going, redirect or take a moment. Whatever you choose, you are still on your way. Go gentle on yourself; don't look for a perfect graph for your life, success isn't linear.

Everybody is unique in their life experience, life stage and how they show up in the world. From neurodivergence to mental-health issues and disabilities, there may be all kinds of challenges that present themselves as you look to make changes in life. Self-compassion and self-exploration are at the core of all you are doing; it's not about succeeding or failing, it's about learning to tweak life so that it flows better for *you*.

Whatever inkling you have about changes you'd like to make in your life or even just something you'd like to give a go, start small, take the first tiny step and back yourself – you never know where it might lead you.

LISTEN TO THE WHISPERS AND THE RAGE

There is no such thing as a 'bad' emotion. As humans, we love to label things, to put them in boxes and contextualise. It helps us to make sense of the world, but it can also limit us when we use black-and-white thinking to view things as either good or bad, and this includes emotions. All emotions are valid and have their place and should be viewed as communication; rather than repress them, we should take notice of what they represent.

When you feel happy, pay attention: What are you doing? Who is with you? Perhaps you are alone but what is it that is bringing this feeling of joy?

Take a moment to think about something that brought you joy recently – close your eyes or settle your gaze and see what comes to mind. It doesn't need to be the big events like a birthday party or wedding, although these are great memories to relive, but the smaller moments – maybe the sun on your face, a walk on the beach, watching a series on Netflix with your partner or getting stuck into a good book. What brought a moment of joy to you lately? What were you doing? Who were you with? How did it make you feel? How can you bring about more of it?

We are often sold the idea that happiness is a permanent state to strive for when, in truth, Ronan Keating was right when he sang about life being a roller-coaster. There are ups and there are downs; happiness comes in moments, make sure to take them in.

What about when you feel sad or angry – what is causing this? For more challenging emotions and darker moods, it may be important to seek professional help from your GP, a therapist or by calling Samaritans, but we all experience down times and it's important to notice these too. Often, it's worth investigating your physical life at that time – have you been sleeping well, eating well, getting out to move your body, connecting with the people in your life? After you've gone through that list, it's worth looking at the other things that are going on in your life that might be contributing to how you feel.

We all get flat days when things feel a bit meh but if you are feeling frustrated and angry, something is causing that. I love the work of Alana Kirk, The Midlife Coach, such as her books

The Sandwich Years and *Midlife, Redefined.* She works mostly with women but her advice applies to all – if it feels hard, it probably is hard. Can you pick apart the threads to find out what the root cause is? Often it seems like we just have to grin and bear certain things – it's just the way life is – but often with some tweaks, some conversations and some support, you can begin to feel different.

Parents are often told that all behaviour from children is communication and I think the same way about our emotions. Treat your emotions with the same compassion that you treat a child's behaviour. Okay, sometimes you want to tear your hair out when you get a call from the school but I truly believe that there is no such thing as bad behaviour and often there is worry, anxiety and sadness, which leads to the child seeking attention. When a child's behaviour is challenging, it can feel hard to show love, but that is when they need our love the most. We are the same – if you are snappy, irritable or even raging, give yourself some love and the space to work things out.

And women, it's not just your hormones – too often we blame different parts of our cycle or chapter in life for our reactions and while these play a role, chances are you need to be seen, heard or helped more. Suss it out and seek the support. If you're not feeling yourself, your energy levels may be low and your mood will be too. Reach out to a friend, a family member, a partner, a colleague – can they help to lighten the load?

This need to listen and validate our emotions is for both genders, or however you identify. Our emotions are sending us a message about what we need in life.

I always say that one of my best health-and-wellness tips is having a GP you can trust. They should also be on your list to discuss how you feel, and 'just not feeling yourself' is enough of a symptom. You don't have to wait until things are really bad and you shouldn't worry about wasting people's time. You deserve to feel good within yourself, however that looks to you, and if that's changed and you've done what you can with your lifestyle, then reach out. Putting your hand up to say you aren't coping and need help isn't a weakness, it's a strength. It shows that you value yourself enough to speak up, and if those around you can't help or things don't change, your GP is the gatekeeper to all kinds of support.

CAN I SAY 'NO'?

Boundaries are an essential part of self-care. Tricky though they may be at times, you need them in place for your life to flow. We all have responsibilities and there are things we have to do that we would prefer not to, but there are also so many things we do because we think we *should*. Lots of us could fall under the category of 'people-pleasers'; it's evolutionary that we want to be liked to survive, but there is no point running ourselves into the ground – that's not a great survival tactic in the long term, is it?

Remember, every time you say 'yes', you are saying 'no' to something else and often that is to yourself – to your time and your energy. Bear that in mind.

You don't have to explain yourself and you don't have to show up to everything, it's okay to say (or even text), 'Sorry, that doesn't suit me' or 'Sorry I can't make that work', or you can tell a white lie that the date, time, etc. doesn't suit – it doesn't suit because you are spending time prioritising yourself, so it's not really a lie.

Some say that 'No' is a full sentence but, for me, that's a little much. I think receiving just *No* back to a text invitation is rather chilling. But you find what works for you.

A friend once said to me that women should text and email like most men do – short and to the point. And, do you know what, I've taken the advice on board. I often catch myself waffling on through paragraph two about why I can't do something or how sorry I am to bother them with my request: 'no worries if not' and other such fluff. I now reread and often I hit delete and start again more succinctly. There is a Goldilocks just-right way to manage this; find yours and go for it.

It can be helpful to ask for more time to think something over – maybe it's a work request or something more personal or social. Ask if you can get back to them and take a beat to work out how saying 'yes' will impact your schedule, family and your other commitments. Don't have your default set to 'yes' every time – I can't help but think that too many yeses lead you right down the path to doormat street, and all you'll find there is overwhelm and burnout. It's great to be social, busy and in demand but everybody has their limit; set yours wisely.

Now, this suggestion is pretty rich coming from me, as I long to be more organised, to be the one leading the days and weeks rather than them leading me. But I assure you that I am trying, as I feel the effects as I whirlwind from one thing to another. What I try to do is look at the week and month ahead and make sure there are not too many yeses. As a self-employed freelancer with a penchant for the high life, two dependents and an animal (the cat, not the husband), it is tricky, let me tell you. Let burnout avoidance be the compass with which you map out your time.

When I get a request or invitation, I start to look not just at the particular date and time in my diary but also what is on in the days leading up to it and after it, and how much energy I will need on those days, and this is what informs my reply. I view my energy and social battery like the tide: sometimes, I am in full flow but then I need to withdraw and recharge. This does not happen unmanaged, you need to schedule downtime, rest time, fun time – whatever it is that recharges you.

Who are you in your life, be it your work life, your home life or your friendship groups? Are you the fixer, the worrier, the carrier, the doer? These are all great people and we all need them in our lives, but you can't be all things to everyone at the expense of your own wellbeing. Often when growing up with our family, we can take on a role that we carry into adulthood – the responsible one, the crazy one, the organiser, the minder. Which one are you? Yes, it's embedded in who you are and may well be a beautifully intentioned, caring role, but what impact is it having on you? Is it lighting you up or is it draining you?

Do you need some support with it? Sometimes, there are situations in our lives that we can't change but we have to get support in managing them better – be that confiding in a friend, a partner or with the help of a therapist.

Our boundaries don't always have to be vocalised either, we can create them in our own psyche, just for us. You don't need to go around telling everybody about your new world order, shouting *No!* to anyone who will listen. Sometimes, it's a quiet mindset, an invisible force field if you will – you know where the boundary is. It can be an end to letting certain people or situations hold power over you and it can feel fantastic. Other times, it can feel more challenging but, ultimately, you will know what is right for you. There are some life situations we can't change, but we can still mind our energy within them, and our reactions.

Get building your fortress, with you and your sanity at the centre, and be mindful of who you let the drawbridge down for.

WELL? OVER TO YOU ...

What's Your Personality Type?

It's worth knowing your personality type to know whether we say 'yes' or 'no' too much or too little. Try this test and see what comes up for you.

The Myers-Briggs Type Indicator® assessment is a tool that helps people to increase their self-awareness, to understand and appreciate differences in others, and to apply personality insights that will improve their personal and professional effectiveness (www.mbtionline.com).

What are you currently saying 'yes' to that you'd like to say 'no' to?

What is stopping you from saying 'no'?

What have you said 'yes' to recently that you regretted? Why?

If you could say 'no' more often, what would you do with the time it would release?

Part 2
BODY

When we think about our bodies, often we think about our physical health, our vital signs and systems that help us function at our best. In this section, I want to focus on the relationship we have with our bodies and how that influences our thoughts, behaviours and, ultimately, our wellbeing.

It might sound bonkers, having a relationship with your own body, but why shouldn't you have one? You need to listen to your body to get a sense of what you need to feel at your best, yet so many of us are disconnected from these signals. I've met many people over the years who put their body down, describing it in negative terms. I sat with a group of beauty therapists at a skincare launch once who told me that a large proportion of women who come for treatments apologise before getting onto the bed, apologise that they haven't shaved or waxed, apologise that their skin is rough and some even said sorry that they had put on weight. I know men are not immune to these feelings of body inadequacy and if you identify outside of the genders, not being comfortable in your own skin or being challenged about your appearance is often par for the course.

My hope is that at the end of this section, you will reach a point of self-acceptance and even love for your body – wherever you are at – just as it is. And please, stop apologising for taking up space.

In my first radio job many years ago, a phone-and-text-in show, there was a caller named Shannon, who I will never forget. She told us of her experience after her gastric-band surgery – she had gone from a size 24 to a size 8 in a matter of months and many of her health markers had improved. She said she had felt invisible before she lost the weight and now that she was a certain size, people were kinder to her, from bus drivers to strangers in the street. This made her sad because she was still the very same person.

In more recent times, I was joined on my current show by Linda. After years of struggling on a fertility journey, she and her husband had to get their heads around not becoming parents, which was understandably tough. She took herself off on a very physically demanding challenge, hiking the snowy mountains of Poland and getting into a freezing cold lake – and she returned a different person. She had felt that her body had failed her, which wasn't a good place to be, but following her experience on the mountain, she had a new-found love and respect for her strong and brilliant body that had got her through, and she felt invincible.

Our relationship with our bodies is complex, but a healthy one is intrinsic to our wellbeing as it informs so many of our thoughts, habits and behaviours.

AT WAR WITH YOUR BODY

I didn't realise for many years that I was at war with my body. I don't remember when it started but there are points along the road that stick out for me. For example, when someone said that I didn't have the body to become a ballerina. I mean, they were probably right and meant no harm but I still remember filing it away in the my-body-is-wrong folder. I remember the magazines of the 1990s glorifying the supermodels – they were spectacular-looking, and still are, but I didn't look like that.

I loved the documentary *The Supermodels* in 2023, it was filled with nostalgia and beauty but also the sad tale of stunning Linda Evangelista being scarred for life by botched cosmetic surgery as she tried to maintain the perfection she was known for. A stark reminder that we rarely know the sacrifice or feelings behind an image in a magazine, but often we still log that image as a standard to aim for.

I don't know when I started comparing my body to other people's. Who had longer legs than me? Or a smaller waist than me? It seems ridiculous even typing that now, but it seeps into your everyday without you even being aware of it. On the street, in a café – anywhere – my eyes would scan to see where I fitted in the pecking order.

I had a boyfriend once who sat scowling in a nightclub and when I asked him what was wrong, he took me home to tell me that he thought I should lose some weight, he felt I could have a better ass than I did. I felt empty. In hindsight, that moment actually empowered me rather than damaged me because I knew what he had said wasn't okay.

My first big love never said anything like that to me, he loved me exactly as I was and laughed when I ate more food than him. Not with any malice, he just wasn't a foodie and I always have been. There was a restaurant that used to serve fry-ups for the hungover and I'd order a bigger one than him, and he'd smile over at me with affection. I never wanted to be that girl who pretended to enjoy salad over chocolate cake – we've come a long way since then (I hope), but that used to be a thing. Why have women spent so long wanting to be thinner? We've been made smaller by so many societal constructs, we don't need to do it to ourselves.

Being in that first big relationship gave me so much, being accepted and valued just as I was became fuel as my body began changing with my new-found love of the gym. I mean, I was twenty-one, still so young, but it was a time of body confidence and acceptance for sure.

There were times I thought that my body wasn't right for a job or a holiday and I would have spent time focusing on weight loss leading up to the event. There were times when I forgot about how lucky I am to have a body that is able and healthy, and that has given me three pregnancies and two babies. I forgot to tune in and listen to the messages it was sending me, from the chronic constipation on a high-protein diet to non-existent periods when my body fat dropped very low in my twenties. I didn't even notice, I just described myself as 'irregular'.

When you stop listening to your body and stop giving it what it needs, you break a sacred connection. Dr Mary Ryan is an endocrinologist who told me of women who book in to see her and arrive weeping and wondering why their hormones are askew and their energy levels are on the floor. When she asks them to talk her through their week, she will often find that they are over-exercising, working in high-powered jobs, doing most of the home responsibilities and trying to juggle it all along with a busy social calendar. They can't imagine slowing down as they are on the treadmill of trying to do it all and be it all, at the expense of their health and wellbeing.

Interoception

Interoception is the ability to be aware of internal sensations, including heart rate, respiration, hunger, fullness, temperature and pain, as well as your emotions as messengers. Our bodies are hard-wired to return to balance or homeostasis, so for example when it needs fuel it sends hunger signals – the idea is that we would feed the body then so it can return to homeostasis.

Interoception can also have a significant impact on our behaviour and emotions. If you're out walking in the dark, you might feel scared and your heart will start beating faster. You may make the decision to return inside or use a torch. By identifying how you feel, interoception helps you decide what to do.

There are two types of interoception as shown on my.clevelandclinic.org:

- **Attention**: How often you notice signals from your body.
- **Accuracy**: How correct you are at understanding signals from your body.

Examples of interoception include:
- A full bladder
- Anxiety or nervousness
- Hot or cold temperatures
- Hunger
- Itchy skin

- Muscle tension
- Nausea
- Thirst
- Pain
- Changes to heartbeat.

Interoception varies from person to person, and neurodivergence and mental-health issues can play a role here. But if you're in a negative space with how you view your body, can you really be in tune with it? What happens when you continually override or ignore your body's messages?

How many times in a relationship have you felt frustrated because you're talking and the other person isn't listening? Do you do that to yourself? What is your body trying to tell you?

There are many factors that contribute to you becoming disconnected from your body and what it needs. Being critical of how it looks is not a very motivating place to start.

You need to start feeling good about yourself. Shifting your focus to self-worth, valuing your health now and into the future, your energy levels, your mental health and your relationship with food and your body is a far stronger starting point than tearing yourself down.

Have you ever experienced that feeling after a holiday or a weekend away when you have thrown all rules out and towards the end you start to feel sluggish and ready for a bit of normality?

That's your body talking to you. The more in tune you become to it, the less of a pendulum swing these things are.

Every body is a beach body, a yoga body, a running body, every body is beautiful just the way it is. Athletic bodies are beautiful, curvy bodies are beautiful.

If you're not quite ready to strip naked, stand in front of the mirror and shout 'I love you' (I have not tried this exercise myself), don't worry – start small. Start listening.

If you feel uncomfortable in a situation, do your best to get out of it, listen, receive the message and then decide what you need to do next. If you're feeling low, what will fill your cup? If you're feeling tired, take a rest.

Lay down your weapons, end the war. Stop speaking to your body with a stream of negativity. Be grateful for all that it does for you. Make peace with your body.

DIETING DOESN'T WORK

This message has become so central to what I deem to be a truly healthy life that I had to dedicate a whole chapter to it. So, one more time for the people at the back: dieting doesn't work. A study of more than 278,000 people found that within five years, the proportion of people who regain all their lost weight (or more) after a diet is between 95 and 98 per cent (Stunkard *et al.*, 1959).

Nutrition is important, that is not in question, but strict rules that you must live by, that involve a transactional relationship between what you consume and what you burn off, is simply not a healthy way to live.

Fildes, Alison *et al.* (2015) noted that the vast majority of people who go on a diet to lose weight will put it all back on – and often more – as soon as they stop their strict calorie-counting. What impact does that have on their mental health, their physical health, their self-esteem, their motivation?

I would question weight loss being a 'health' goal on its own. Just because someone weighs a certain number on the scales does not necessarily mean they are healthier than someone of another weight, particularly when we take into account the pillars of wellbeing – movement, nutrition, stress management, rest and connection. If someone ignores all of those yet fits within the healthy body mass index (BMI) range, are they healthier than someone outside of the range who moves daily, eats well, manages their stress and sleeps well? It just doesn't add up, it's far more complex than that. I prefer a focus on a healthy relationship with food and body as the number one goal; everything that happens after that is a bonus.

Our bodies also have a set-point weight, a homeostasis or equilibrium that it will try to get back to. Our weight is not just determined by diet and exercise but also genetics and our environment. The 'eat less, move more' theory is outdated and incorrect (Ganipisetti & Bollimunta, 2025).

If I could go back to parenting really small kids again, one thing I would definitely like to do is change the language I used around food. When you know better, you do better, as they say. My intentions at the time were, of course, good, but I labelled foods as being 'good' or 'bad', I put certain 'treat' foods up on a pedestal, I said things like, 'If you finish everything on your plate and eat all your vegetables, you can get ice cream.' These are things that were said to us as children and again, the intention was to have us focus on the foods that helped us grow and minimise the foods that were simply fun.

However, we are all born with an innate sense of our own appetite and what we need. When we constantly undermine and override that, it can erode that inner dialogue and inner knowing. My kids were often the ones still at the sweet table at a birthday party when all the other kids were on the bouncy castle. I made beetroot brownies for their own first birthday parties but when they had tasted the real-chocolate deal, they began to hand me back the less sugary snacks. It is a tough line to tread – the amount of sugar on offer to our kids these days is tenfold what it was when we were young and, as a parent, there is an instinct that kicks in to feed and protect your child, but there are other elements that deserve safeguarding too.

Like my kids at a birthday party, I often found myself like a grown-up child at lots of tables. Constantly restricting calories in the week often meant that when the floodgates were opened – out for dinner or eating takeaway – I found it hard to stop. It was as if I didn't know when I would be able to eat like this again, so I stocked up. The converse is that when you throw away food and dieting rules, when there is no limit on when you might be able to eat and how much, you begin to settle into an inner knowing of what you need, and that's often not what you think it is.

'Intuitive eating' is a concept developed by Evelyn Tribole and Elyse Resch in the 1990s. They are both registered dieticians and eating-disorder specialists and, having seen the damage caused by dieting, they wanted to give people a better message around their relationship with food. They devised a ten-step programme but perhaps the most pertinent steps are to reject diet culture and make peace with the food and drink you consume. When this becomes the way you live, you can free up so much more space in your head to find out what it is you need and how you can truly nourish yourself.

This may be a massive mindset shift for you – it was for me. Often, we hold on to ways of living so tightly that to let them go feels like the wheels will come off our lives and we will spin out of control.

But have you ever stopped to consider the impact so much control has on you?

Of course, it is true that food is there to fuel and sustain us, but it also serves as a way for us to connect with ourselves and others. We attach so many of our emotional experiences to food, from being fed and bonding as a baby, to celebrating with cake at a party, to bringing food to a wake. We often demonise comfort eating, but food can be comforting.

When you make this peace with food, you are committing to having a healthy relationship with it, accepting that the relationship you've had with it up until now perhaps needed to change. Everyone assumes that when the rules are taken away, wild abandon will follow. You will live on a diet of all the foods you now consider 'bad' or 'treats', and you will trade in your work and social life for the biscuit tin. The reality is that while there might be a settling-in period, things do settle down and you begin to listen to your body and what it needs. When you turn down all the other noise, you figure out that you need more than a constant stream of biscuits.

Also, who said that constantly cutting calories was healthy? That you should cut out certain food groups and risk undernourishing your body? Having a constant stream of stress around what you eat and how you look, permeating your every thought, is not good for your health. Yo-yoing from a strict diet to eating everything you want and berating yourself in between – again, not optimum health.

One of the most dangerous aspects of diet culture is that it stands in the way of people getting the healthcare they need. It perpetuates eating practices that have real mental and physical health consequences while simultaneously putting the blame for any health issues on the individual's body size.

The thing with dieting and a focus on weight loss alone is that while the scales might say what you want them to for a certain amount of time, what matters is whether or not you reached your goal weight in a healthy way. Did unhealthy behaviours lead you there?

Constant dieting can wreak havoc with your mental health and damage your metabolism in the long term as your body struggles to cope with what it often deems to be a time of starvation and depravation. It begins to go into self-preservation mode and hold on to calories.

I don't demonise weight loss or having an intention to lose some weight, but only if it involves healthy measures and comes with self-worth over self-loathing. My preferred focus would be on improving the relationship that you have with food and your body, making small and consistent lifestyle changes that make you feel good. Increased energy levels, better mood, better sleep, greater connections and just feeling good in your own skin are all more favourable motivators than a target weight or clothes size. Perhaps bringing these changes in will result in weight loss but I'd prefer it was an add on rather than a sole focus.

I believe that people come in all different shapes and sizes, that you don't have to look a certain way to be healthy and that life is too short to spend it wishing you looked different. When you put your own self-worth and truly nourish yourself – mind, body and soul at the centre of your wellbeing – for me, that's the best body to be in.

WELL? OVER TO YOU ...

Use your answers to the following statements, adapted from www.eatingwisdom.com, to reflect on your relationship with food and your body. (Use a scale of 1 to 10 where 1 is 'never' and 10 is 'always'.)

I am interested in food.

It's a mood-lifter when I've lost weight.

I exercise to burn calories or change my body.

I feel guilty when eating 'treat' foods.

I can stop eating when full.

I always gain weight on holiday.

I eat all kinds of foods.

WOULD YOU BE WELL?

I'm upset if I gain weight.

I think about my weight and body shape.

I think about nutrition but also taste and enjoyment.

I think about burning off or getting rid of calories after eating.

I trust my body when it comes to food and weight management.

I enjoy feeling hungry.

I eat differently when I'm by myself.

I love my body.

If any red flags emerge from the answers you have given to these questions, please seek support. As we've discussed, it can be challenging to rewire long-term behaviours and attitudes but it is not impossible. There have been so many factors, some that will be outside of your control, which have led you here so there should be no guilt, blame or shame. With the right support you can begin to heal your relationship with your body and food.

I would recommend:
- www.carlabredin.ie
- www.nutritionwithniamh.com Niamh's book *No Apologies* is excellent
- www.bodywhys.ie
- www.instagram.com/intuitive.eating.ireland.

HOLDING IN YOUR TUMMY

A yoga teacher from South Africa came to live in my village a few years ago. A beautiful ball of energy, she lit up the place as she embraced the community, jumped into our cold sea, drove her pick-up with her blond-haired toddler and held the most incredible events and classes. On a Thursday evening, she gave a yin yoga class where she would get us into stretch-out postures that we would hold for minutes at a time with a focus on letting go.

I've never met anyone with an energy like hers, she had almost a perfect symmetry of yin-and-yang energy, strong and gentle in open view. She would forcefully remind us to bring our minds back to the present moment with her strong voice, all while laying blankets and eye pillows on us. She would command our attention and hold a gentle space for us in equal measure. I loved that class. You would arrive, head swimming with thoughts from the day and what was to come. You dared not arrive late or you weren't allowed in. There was no idle chit-chat on the mat before the class began – the curtains were drawn, the candles were lit, the incense was burning, and it was a safe space to simply relax and let go.

Through the course of the class, as with many other classes, you would find yourself moving away from a focus on your mind back down into your body. She would have you focusing on your jaw, your hip bones … parts of my body I never gave a moment's thought to would be attended to and encouraged to relax. It was an intense but amazing experience and we would all float out of there full of appreciation about who we are when we truly relaxed.

During that class, I had a realisation that surprised me. The tummy was an area she would give much focus to, telling us to let it go, like a Buddha. I really struggled with this, to the point that I'm not sure I ever really could say with confidence that I did it. I recognised that I had spent so many years sucking it in that it was virtually impossible for my brain to compute doing anything different.

Who on earth have I been holding in my tummy for?

When I was pregnant, some friends got married on New Year's Eve. I love a wedding at that time of year as it's a lovely way to ring in the new year – and I was designated driver so no taxi-out-of-town head-wreck.

I love the mingling at a wedding and was chatting at our table. Then, as I got up to go to the bathroom, I went to suck in my tummy. I was wearing a tight, black-lace maternity number but I forgot for a moment that I was sporting a bump. I remember feeling joy that I didn't have to suck in my tummy for however many more months of pregnancy I had left. I mean, how sad is that? And don't get me started on the putting of the hand on the hip to keep your arm away from your body in photos lest anyone sees there is flesh there – it's sad to see how many of us ask for digital photos to be deleted or taken again.

I suppose I've the slowing down of that yin yoga class to thank for making me realise that I've been clutching in my tummy for far too long.

Who set the body standard? It may or may not surprise you to learn that diet culture was designed by the patriarchy to help hold women back. Women's bodies have been objectified, scrutinised and policed throughout history, as patriarchal systems have sought to control and regulate women's autonomy. Diet culture perpetuates the idea that women must be thin, in order to be valued and accepted.

Throughout the ages, women went from being revered to being controlled. During the 1500s and 1600s, the corset that we know today began to gain in popularity, idealising the image of a small waist. In the 1700s, corsets also aimed to improve posture. They were fitted with shoulder straps that would force the shoulders back so far that the shoulder blades would touch.

Nineteenth-century corsets emphasised a more hourglass shape and were more focused on shrinking the waist than previous corsets had been, in the process often damaging to a woman's skin and inner organs.

This attitude can still be seen today with shapewear and waist trainers being worn by Instagram and reality TV's most famous star Kim Kardashian, with her booming company also suggesting headpieces to be worn overnight for a 'snatched' jawline. They sold out within hours.

Who is setting the beauty standards?

Who is living by them?

Imagine if, instead of spending so much headspace wanting our bodies to be different than they are, we used that energy to stand in our own power. How much time has been wasted trying to keep ourselves small – literally and figuratively? There is no need for any of us to want to be smaller, to shrink and fit into some body ideal that was served up to us, especially if it is unhealthy behaviours that take us there.

Diet culture keeps us focused on changing our bodies instead of changing the world. As Naomi Wolf states in *The Beauty Myth*:

A culture fixated on female thinness is not an obsession about female beauty, but an obsession about female obedience. Dieting is the most potent political sedative in women's history; a quietly mad population is a tractable one.

Thankfully, in more recent times, there has been a move towards making different body ideals more visible. There's a difference in advertising campaigns, on magazine covers and on shop mannequins. There is more body diversity and a move away from flawless filters, but it's still a massive over-focus on the body. I'm all for women embracing fashion and make-up and whatever they rock to feel beautiful, but there is still far too much credence given to a beauty ideal. Even though we have begun to call out impossible beauty standards more, they still exist and can be so limiting – beauty comes in all different shapes, sizes and forms, there should be no ideal.

I take umbrage with the notion of 'body positivity'. I fully appreciate its sentiment, but it's patronising in its message that you should remain positive 'even though' you're in a bigger body. No thanks. I sat beside a brilliantly smart, funny and beautiful woman at a business-awards dinner recently who talked candidly about having always been in a bigger body regardless of how she ate or exercised. She was a qualified personal trainer, Pilates instructor and had been a dancer, but even though her sisters didn't share her obsession with movement, they could eat whatever they liked and remain thin. Sometimes, it is just the body we are born with rather than the choices we make.

She said she had recently been on holiday with a group of women and many of them had felt it was complimentary to tell her how brave she'd been to wear a bikini on the beach and by the pool. It was well intentioned, sure, but it was also offensive to consider her valiant for just doing what everybody else was doing. Was she brave because her body shape wasn't okay for bikinis but she'd worn one anyway? She also told me that when she was asked to be an ambassador for a very famous athleisure brand, her size was never in stock. The bigger the size, the more fabric is required and more panels are required so it's more labour-intensive. Brands say they are inclusive but not at the expense of their profit margins.

It works both ways. My sister is naturally slim and over the years has had derogatory comments sent her way questioning her eating habits. We don't have any right to comment on other people's bodies or to judge them.

I prefer to champion body neutrality, a focus on being healthy rather than looking a certain way. There are times I want to share a video on Instagram talking about tummy rolls or stretch marks; I do appreciate them when I see these videos from others, but I still think it's just too much focus on the body.

Who are you keeping yourself small for? Who are you holding your tummy in for? What is it holding you back from?

A study from personal care brand Dove found that 75 per cent of women and 65 per cent of girls had opted out of activities such as school events, sports and other social engagements because of concerns about their appearance.

When I worked in television, I would hear from producers of news panel shows that it was easier to fill the slots with male contributors last minute than it was female. The reasons for this may be many, some of which may include women carrying more of the load in the home despite advances in equality, but I think part of it is down to the fact that many women would find it hard to go on television without being ready with their appearance and being fully prepared with what they had to say.

To be full of yourself is often considered a negative thing but what's the alternative – to be empty of yourself? We don't have to be arrogant or rude but let's shine our light, not dim it or try to make it into something else.

One of the biggest trends in recent years is weight-loss injections. While there are many people who have benefitted from this medication, there are still so many unanswered questions. I interviewed the brilliant writer Johann Hari about his book *Magic Pill*, in which he outlines his experience with Ozempic and the risks associated with the drug. He told me about his loss of appetite, how after four bites of his chosen meal he has to throw it away. He spoke of the joy of food as well as his emotional crutch being gone. Are people being supported enough through this transition or are they just supposed to be happy that they fit an ideal?

People have the right to change their body if they wish – hair dye, weightlifting, weight-loss injections, corsets and cosmetic surgery – but a strong sense of self-worth needs to be at the centre of how we view ourselves. It informs so many of our daily decisions and habits that, in turn, influence our health and wellbeing. I don't demonise weight loss by any means but only if it's in tandem with healthy behaviours.

My beautiful yoga friend took her energy to Spain; her time in our chillier seas had run its course. She's returning soon to hold a retreat and I'm booked in. I'll aim for a Buddha belly and I won't be sorry for it.

WELL? OVER TO YOU ...

How would you rate your current relationship with your body? (Use a scale of 1 to 10 where 1 is 'poor' and 10 is 'excellent'.)

What would you like to change about your body?

Why?

What difference do you think it would make to your life if these changes were to happen?

How connected is your relationship to your body and your relationship with food?

What body image ideas did you pick up as a child and teen?

Where did this messaging come from?

If you're not already there, what do you think it will take for you to be happy with your body?

What's one step you could take to improve your relationship with your body?

SENSES AND SENSUALITY

Sounds like a raunchy version of the Jane Austen classic! Why is it that when we hear the word 'sensual' often the first thing we go to in our heads is sex? Yes, the two are linked but to be sensual is to be in your senses – sight, sound, taste, touch and smell. We often hear the phrase 'come out of your head and into your body' but this can be a challenging concept to understand and put into practice. Put simply, your body is always in the present moment, so to become conscious of any of your five senses will bring you into the present moment and can have a calming effect.

We've talked about mindfulness and meditation and if you still find it overwhelming to bring these into your everyday life, I recommend you start with the following.

Try it now, wherever you are reading this (or listening to the audiobook). Are you sitting down? Can you feel your back against the chair or the sofa? Place your two feet on the ground, just for a moment. Bring awareness to your breath and just feel the air coming in and out of your body. Become aware of the sounds around you, those in your immediate environment and those farther away. This is a great exercise to do outside, so in your garden or balcony or when you are on a walk, listen to the birds singing, the wind in the trees, the traffic driving by – just listen to it.

Smell is a fantastic sense that can connect us to memory and feeling. I'm not sure who gave me the tip to get a perfume that I had never worn before for my wedding day but it was one of the best things I ever did. I save that perfume now rather than wear it every day, and when I spritz it on it brings me right back, not just to my wedding day but to that time and our honeymoon. It gives me a great feeling. If our relationship is in a rut, as can happen, I will often give that perfume a spray to get the good vibes going again! Smell is so powerful, so become aware of what you can smell around you. Food, sunscreen, freshly cut grass – so many scents and smells conjure up so many memories and can transport us back. Taking in the scents in the present moment can be very mindful. I love essential oils, incense and candles to set a relaxing mood.

It's so important to be able to come into our bodies and truly feel what is happening within us and around us but this takes practice, a metaphorical muscle that you need to flex so that it will get stronger over time.

We operate in a productivity mindset, always planning and doing, so much so that we forget the importance of the pleasure mindset – to enjoy what it is we are doing, to seek pleasure. 'Pleasure' is a word often saved only for sex and food, and it is worth exploring your own relationship with both. We have basic human needs for both of these and yet there is so much guilt and shame associated with them too. Are you stopping yourself from accessing pleasure in your life and your body? From truly feeling? Are you present with the people around you? Feeling into every experience? Whether it's feeling the grass under your feet, your toes in the sand, the waves that lap around you, the water in the shower on your back, your duvet on you at night, the cuddles of your kids, the hand of your partner – are you tuning in to your own body and the signals it is giving you?

Come out of your head and into your body. Start small with a meditation practice, like the one outlined on the previous page, and lean in to what gives your body pleasure.

EAT UP

OK, now that I've got all that body-image stuff off my chest (pun intended!), let's talk about food.

We have looked in detail at diet culture and are aware of the dangers of eating disorders, but an obsession with 'clean' and 'healthy' eating is also a dangerous place to be.

It is important to be aware of how food nourishes you and helps you to function at your best, but also to have flexibility around what you eat. We all have different appetites, likes and dislikes, family history with food, and different hunger and satiety levels. We are constantly sold this one-size-fits-all approach, and it's just not practical.

The first thing to do is to throw away rules and stress when it comes to how you eat. Kick guilt and shame out too. You could be nailing your nutrition but if you are stressed during the process and constantly beating yourself up, then you may be unravelling much of your good work. Food deserves to be enjoyed, shared and used to bring people together. Since time began, we have gathered together for meals, made use of what we had, fed our bodies and connected with the people around us.

Food is intrinsically linked to our emotions, and comfort eating shouldn't necessarily be feared. Food *is* comforting – a bowl of stew and mashed potato on a cold, wintery day, tomato soup with a cheese toastie when you come in soaked to the skin because you forgot your umbrella, an ice cream cone on a hot, sunny day. Food is tied to our emotions – cake on your birthday, chicken noodle soup when you're coming around after an illness, a dinner you loved as a child, a tub of ice cream and a spoon when you're heartbroken, all are linked to a feeling and a type of healing. The only issue is when food is the only coping skill you use to deal with your emotions. Often, our relationship with food is a symptom of unresolved trauma and the relief doesn't last, so the cycle continues. Again, with professional help from a counsellor, you can change your relationship with food.

I had to work on my own relationship with food and it didn't happen overnight but, as I mentioned earlier, something inside me clicked when I heard performance nutritionist Daniel Davey talk about lean muscle mass as a key indicator of how long you will live and how healthy you will be. He advised me to focus on eating balanced meals, meaning protein, fat and carbohydrates in every one – I couldn't believe how much my energy levels changed. I didn't obsess over anything or weigh anything, but I remember how my shoulders came down as I didn't have to stress or feel guilty about food anymore. Carbs were no longer demonised but welcomed, the same with healthy fats, and I loved shifting focus from what I was taking away to what I was adding in.

So, I'd make, say, a chicken breast, baked potato and a salad, and I'd see that fats were missing so I'd drizzle olive oil, add avocado or sprinkle seeds on top. That sounds like a very virtuous meal, but it's just an example. There was pizza, curry, whatever was going really. I tried new recipes, new ways of cooking – it was the pandemic so there was time to experiment in the kitchen – and while my body did change initially with the new way of eating, eventually I settled into my optimum weight. I don't know what that is as I threw out my scales. Weight wasn't my motivator, I had long moved from a focus on how I looked to how I felt.

There was one day when I slipped back into my old habits, purely without thinking. I was grabbing lunch on the go, as I often did, and I went into a salad bar. I ordered what was basically leaves and veg, the thought loop came back that this was a great low-calorie meal and in the moment I forgot all about the carbs and the protein. I headed home, ate a decent dinner and went to bed. The next morning, I felt exhausted and I tracked it back to not eating enough the day before. I promise you, I don't like to think of food as fuel as it screams gym obsessed and seems joyless but, honestly, when you start to fuel your body correctly you feel better, you sleep better, your brain fog reduces and you feel more motivated to move your body – everything improves.

When I began my training as a health coach, we were taught about that sweet spot between knowing how powerful nutrition can be and the importance of a healthy relationship with your food choices. There has to be balance, flexibility and fun.

With all that in mind, here's the basics on what to consider when it comes to your plate:

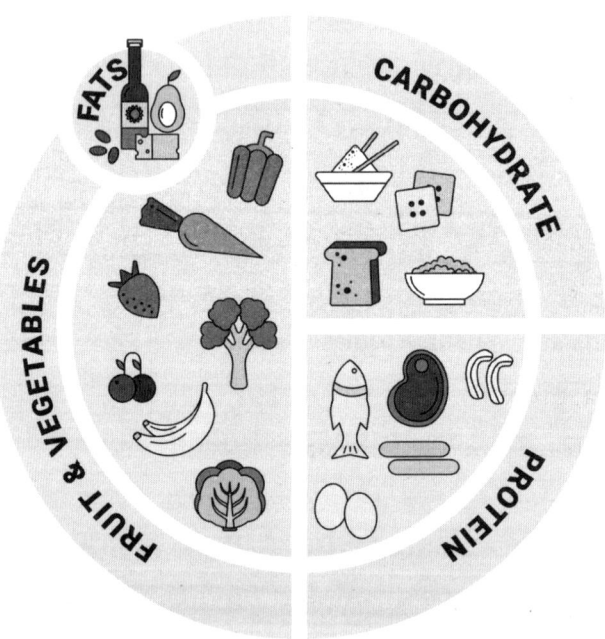

Figure 3: Food groups

Fruit and veg

Fill your plate with lots of vegetables and fruit. These offer so many vitamins, minerals, antioxidants and fibre! Vegetables and fruits are nutritious whether they are purchased fresh, frozen, dried or in cans.

Protein

Protein helps to keep you full for longer, stabilises blood sugars, and maintains and builds muscle and other tissues. Protein can be found in animal-based foods like meat, poultry, fish and eggs, and in dairy or plant-based options like tofu, tempeh, and beans and lentils. Some examples of protein-rich foods include:

- Meat (beef, , pork, game)
- Poultry (chicken, turkey)
- Seafood
- Eggs
- Dairy (Greek yogurt, cottage cheese, milk, whey powders, cheese)
- Beans and lentils (canned beans, dried beans, bean or lentil pasta, protein powders)
- Soy (tofu, tempeh, edamame, soy milk)

It's important to note that foods beyond the list above may provide protein but in smaller amounts. For example, peanut butter, nuts, seeds and wholegrain breads contain some protein!

Carbs

Carbohydrates are crucial for providing the body with energy, particularly for the brain and muscles, and they also play a role in digestion and overall health. They are the body's primary source of fuel, broken down into glucose for immediate energy use or stored for later. Choosing wholegrain or brown varieties provides more fibre than the white options.

- Grains, bread, oats, quinoa, rice, popcorn, cereals, pasta.
- Starchy vegetables (potatoes, sweet potatoes, corn, butternut squash).
- Beans and lentils.

Fats

Fats provide a source of energy, keep you feeling full for longer, regulate blood sugars, enhance the absorption of certain vitamins (A, D, E and K), and are involved in the production of hormones. Fats also provide essential fatty acids that the body cannot produce itself and are vital for a healthy nervous-system function.

You need to eat fat for your brain because the brain is composed of about 60 per cent fat, which is essential for its structure and function, especially for cell membranes and communication between neurons. Healthy fats, particularly omega-3s like DHA, are vital building blocks for brain cells, supporting memory, learning and development from the womb through childhood. Consuming enough healthy fats can improve cell function, reduce inflammation, and may even offer protection against cognitive decline and neurodegenerative diseases.

Although fats can come from certain meat cuts and oily fish, other examples of fat sources include:

- Nuts and nut butters
- Seeds and seed butters (tahini)
- Dairy (cheese, yogurts, sour cream)
- Oils and fats (olive oil, coconut oil, butter, rapeseed oil)
- Avocado, coconut milk.

The fats we want to avoid where possible are trans fats, found in ultra-processed foods, and certain types of saturated fats. Too much saturated fat – found in dairy from butter and cream, coconut, and fattier cuts of meat sources – can increase cholesterol levels, which increases the risk of cholesterol building up in your blood vessels, potentially leading to a heart attack or stroke. Most unsaturated fats come from plant sources and, as you can see from the plate diagram, we need them but we don't need a lot (Wexner Medical Centre; NHS; Saskatchewan Blue Cross).

WELL? OVER TO YOU ...

How would you describe your relationship with food? (Use a scale of 1 to 10 where 1 is 'very poor' and 10 is 'excellent'.)

Do you categorise foods as good or bad?

Can you list these foods? Which are 'good'? Which are 'bad'?

Do you have rules around food and eating?

How often are you counting calories or on a diet?

What impact has this had on your life?

How much value do you place on what your body weighs, or on weight loss?

How do you think you might improve your relationship with food?

If you are happy with where you are at with food – what is working for you?

GUT HEALTH

The emerging science of gut health and our microbiome really cemented my nutrition approach and helped strengthen my focus on adding in rather than taking away. Our microbiome is at the cutting edge of the latest health research and is beginning to be looked on by scientists as almost another organ and the gut as our second brain. There is a constant stream of messages going from our gut to our brain and when our gut is in balance we have better energy levels, a stronger immune system and better moods – 90 per cent of serotonin is made in the gut, so you can literally feed your good mood.

When your gut is out of balance, it is known as 'dysbiosis' and symptoms include low mood and energy levels, a sluggish or overactive bowel, skin issues and general lethargy. When our gut is in balance it enables the body to absorb the nutrients from the food we eat.

The gut microbiome is an incredible collection of bacteria that work for us, but we need to feed them. In fact, our entire body is a collection of systems that rely on nutrients to function at their best. The science is emerging and amazing but what's really important is that you start to think about what you are giving your body to function at its best. I like to think of the microbiome as the sorting office for the nutrients you are taking in – it decides what goes where. The modern food chain will often contain ingredients that our sorting office doesn't recognise and can cause it to malfunction.

The wall of our gut lining is 1 to 2 mm thick so the nutrients can pass into our bloodstream, but factors such as a poor diet, excessive alcohol and stress can cause disruption between the cell walls, enabling harmful substances to leak into the bloodstream, triggering immune responses and other health issues.

We are also too sterile in this modern world, so consider this permission to lay off the housework for the sake of your microbiome! Here are the things your microbiome loves that will improve your gut health.

- **Colour**: Eat the rainbow; see how much colour you can pack into your trolley and onto your plate. If that is overwhelming, consider soups or smoothies, blend up lots of different types of fruit, vegetables, nuts and seeds. Focus on fibre.

- **Diversity**: We can get so stuck in a rut buying the same food every week, that leaves us eating the same meals over and over. I once had an Instagram series about the same five dinners because that was where I was. I wouldn't say I'm streets ahead of that now, and I've definitely destroyed my kids' relationship with green beans (I still love them), but I focus more on mixing it up and trying new recipes for sure.

  It is suggested that we should eat thirty diverse plants per week, which sounds like we need to go munching through the rainforest when, in reality, so many everyday foods are plants.
- **Fibre**: The gut loves fibre, so be sure to have a diet rich in wholegrains (oats, wheat, barley), fresh or frozen fruit and vegetables and legumes (peas, beans and lentils).
- **Herbs and spices**: These are plants too so experiment with adding them to your meals and look for mixes to increase the diversity even more.
- **Nuts and seeds**: Also plants – again, mixed versions provide more diversity.

Start throwing in more with each meal. I often give the example of eating porridge in the morning, adding a fruit compote (frozen mixed berries, mixed spice and chia seeds boiled in a pot) with flaked almonds on the top and you are at nine plants already. It's the focus on what you are adding in that I think is such an important mindset shift. Instead of counting calories, count nutrients.

- **Fermented foods**: Kimchi, miso paste/soup, tempeh, kombucha, kefir, kraut or vegetables – these products should be live and found in the fridge. Most supermarkets have them and we have lots of amazing Irish producers.

Look up recipes for them and just add them in – fermented kraut or cabbage works well with eggs and toast, you can get fermented hot sauce too, you can add the kraut or veg to wraps and sandwiches. There is a sharp taste that you actually start to crave the more you eat it. Drinking kefir, kombucha or miso soup is easier if that's more your thing.

Yogurt with live/active cultures can also work and is a great vehicle for the gut-friendly grains, fruits, nuts and seeds. Be wary of claims on labels as so many are jumping on the gut-health bandwagon – just because it says gut health on the label doesn't mean it's true; approach headline statements on labels with caution.

Fermented foods provide probiotics and there are also prebiotics in garlic, onions and other vegetables. You don't need to overthink things, just focus on diversity, colour and dabble in fermented foods if you don't already, and see how you get on.

Consuming too many sugars, additives or preservatives isn't great for your gut, and it's important to consider a probiotic supplement to repopulate the good bacteria in your gut after you've taken an antibiotic, but it's also important that you don't stress too much about these things. It's best to adopt a crowding-out mentality: by including as many nourishing foods as possible, you will begin to crowd out those that aren't as good for you, but this will evolve over time rather than in a stressed and forced way.

When you start to notice the changes in how you feel, it will become easier to make the choices that make you feel good and still allow space for those moments of convenience or fun.

I was listening to a podcast interview with a former alcoholic and drug addict who was saying her tolerance had completely changed – she now feels hungover after a Chinese takeaway, which made me laugh. When you eat in a more intuitive and nourishing way, banning rules and stress, it self-perpetuates and eventually becomes who you are and how you live. You get hooked on feeling good!

Focusing on nourishing your body is a mindset shift you won't regret and gut health is a great place to start.

MOVEMENT

I want to start a movement, about movement. I think we need to rebrand exercise and simply call it 'movement'. The word 'exercise' can be intimidating and bring up memories of PE kits and hard work; movement sounds a lot more doable, even if it does make me think of contemporary dance or doing a poo. The important part is not how you move but that you make time for movement in your everyday life.

There are so many new trends in 'exercise' – CrossFit has now been eclipsed somewhat by HYROX, there are more people than ever before entering competitions and making it a city break across Europe. The exercise stalwarts remain, of course – the gym, spin classes, yoga and Pilates, with reformer very much having a moment. There also seem to be more people running, with running clubs springing up all over the place as the new way to socialise while you get healthy. All of this is fantastic.

When you find something you love to do, that's the golden ticket. When you do something because you feel you have to, because you hate your body and you need to lose weight or tone up – well, that is a buzz kill for life.

Moving your body not only helps all the systems in your body to flow (I realise that again sounds like I mean toilet, but that too), it improves your sleep and gives you more energy – which can seem like a contradiction – and it's incredible for your mental health.

The word 'emotion' is basically energy in motion and if you're stressing over something and head out for a walk, you often come back with the answer or you feel slightly better because you moved, you worked through it.

Then, there is the endorphin release, the fact you showed up for yourself, chances are you got out of the house – it's a double whammy if you got out in nature – and your body, mind and spirit will thank you for it now and in the future.

So, now, you just need to find your particular jam. If you don't like the gym, don't go! Don't make yourself do anything because you feel you have to, try on all the movement hats until you find something you enjoy and even if none of them fit, just walk around your neighbourhood or your garden, do some simple movements at home. But move – your body loves it.

Remember the blue zones around the world where people live longest and healthiest, with many over the age of a hundred in good physical and cognitive health? Simple movement is part of their everyday lives. They don't have personal trainers or gym memberships but they walk around where they live, they move every day.

Get outside. There is lots of research around how blue and green spaces can relax and calm us so seek them out. They can reduce feelings of tension, fatigue and stress, improving our overall mood. Epidemiological studies have identified associations between living in greener or coastal areas and greater health outcomes (Smith & others, 2011).

It's a major bugbear of mine that not enough heed is paid to this research when it comes to town planning, particularly in urban areas and city centres – green spaces should be prioritised and accessible for all. They're essential to our health and wellbeing.

A recent UK study of nearly 20,000 people (Abookire, 2020) showed that spending at least 120 minutes a week in nature improved self-reported health and wellbeing. These two hours can be broken down into blocks throughout the week, even ten to fifteen minutes a day can make a difference. So if you can take your movement outside, do it.

For now, focus on movement – where is it showing up in your day and week? Can you add some in – take the stairs over the lift, a walk in the evening with a neighbour, a class you've always wanted to try? It can be walking, bowling, dancing, swimming, gardening, stretching, running, weightlifting – just move, your body will thank you for it.

WELL? OVER TO YOU ...

How do you like to move your body? Going for a walk? Going to the gym? Dancing to a song on the radio? Doing gentle stretches while you're sitting down?

How often do you move your body?

Is there a type of movement that you'd like to try? A class, a hike or something online?

What is currently making it challenging for you to increase the amount of movement in your day or week?

What might change this?

If you are currently exercising regularly – do you enjoy it? (Yes, a challenge is important but so is enjoyment.)

If the answer is 'no', are there changes you could make for it to be more enjoyable? Perhaps with a friend, a class closer to home, online, something more relaxed like yoga or Pilates. Maybe look at how often you are outdoors and in nature, or return to something you loved as a child, such as swimming or dance.

REST AND RECHARGE

In our modern lives, we are obsessed with doing and productivity. Social media is awash with people getting up in the middle of the night so that they have meditated, worked out, batch-cooked and swallowed a vat of supplements, all before dawn.

We are not getting enough rest. Part of me feels that we are hyper-focusing on sleep and stressing about rest, which is counterintuitive, but restorative practice is such an important component of our health and wellbeing.

So what does good rest look like? Is it doing nothing? It's such a tricky concept for us to get our heads around but, yes, doing absolutely nothing. Is it relaxing to watch a streamed series? Yes, and it's nice to scroll through our feed from time to time, but do these things really restore us? We are taking in so much information – the plots of various dramas, soap operas and real-life crime – but how much attention are we paying to our own storyline? Can you sit and simply be? Do you give yourself the opportunity to truly rest and recharge?

As with so much of health and wellbeing, we essentially know what we need to be doing, but it's the execution of it that is the tricky part. We don't have time – time to move, time to eat well, time to rest – and while, yes, life is busy, you need to find the time to invest in yourself, to take care of yourself, to prioritise yourself. It helps you to do everything better.

The red-light district

One of the best ways to think about rest is to consider your central nervous system, which plays a crucial role in the fight-or-flight response by triggering the sympathetic nervous system to prepare the body for perceived threats. This response, also known as the acute stress response, involves a cascade of physiological changes that enable an individual to either confront or escape danger.

The sympathetic nervous system initiates the fight-or-flight response by releasing adrenaline and other hormones. These hormones cause a series of physical changes, including:

- **Increased heart rate and blood pressure**: To pump blood and oxygen to muscles more efficiently.
- **Muscle tension**: To prepare the body for physical action.
- **Rapid breathing**: To increase oxygen intake for energy production.

- **Pupil dilation**: To improve vision and focus on the perceived threat.
- **Suppressed digestion**: To divert energy to more critical functions.
- **Release of glucose**: For a quick energy boost.

When the threat has passed, the parasympathetic nervous system counteracts the sympathetic nervous system, returning the body to a resting state known as rest and digest.

Freeze (to do nothing in the moment) and fawn (similar to freeze but more appeasing in nature) are both used to protect us in the midst of a traumatic experience, and are also important stress responses. However, for the purpose of this chapter, we are going to focus on fight or flight and rest and digest.

Our systems have not evolved very much from our cave-dwelling existence, what has changed is the world around us. The central nervous system came in rather handy when our ancestors ventured out of the cave to hunt and gather or just to explore – an unexpected noise or even coming into contact with a wild animal and the central nervous system would kick in to allow a sprint back to the cave and safety, where the heart rate would come back down and rest and digest would return.

The issue today is that the 'always on' culture means that we are often in a state of chronic stress for long periods of time due to the demands that are placed upon us. Our central nervous system doesn't know that we're running from a to-do list or hundreds of WhatsApp messages but the reaction is the same. If we stay in fight-or-flight mode without returning to rest and digest then it has an impact on all our bodily functions; we can't operate at our optimum when we are primed for danger. Digestion, fertility, hormonal, mental and physical health all require restorative rest. In the same way that our laptops and smart devices need to shut down and reboot, so do we.

There are many elements outside of your control which can cause you to be in fight or flight – our lean towards productivity, the need for two-income households, the cost of living crisis, the housing crisis, climate change, the 'always on' connected world. It's no wonder we struggle to wind down but it's important to focus on what you can – taking measures that suit you to bring yourself back to rest and digest whenever you can.

I often work with a brilliant psychotherapist, Nicole Paulie, and she gave me the analogy of our stress levels being like a water bottle. Stress is inevitable in our life, we can take steps to reduce its impact but we'll never avoid it completely. So picture the empty water bottle with every life stress adding a little more water each time. If we are not taking measures to reduce the amount of water/stress then it will continue to fill right up to the top – the bigger the stress, the more water goes in until it's so close to the top that any stress, no matter how minor, such as someone cutting you off in traffic or being put on hold, will push your bottle to overflowing and your reactions will be bigger, as will the impact on your wellbeing.

So, how do you know what works for you when it comes to relieving your stress and releasing that water? A couple of years ago, I was contacted by Janine van Someren who, along with husband Ken, runs The Wellbeing Advantage. They both hold PhDs in human performance and, after working with professional athletes at the elite level, they began to work with corporate leaders. Janine contacted me at a time when they wanted to bring their wealth of knowledge to everyone, to help people realise their true potential and performance, away from elite sport and the top management and they asked if I'd do a piece on my radio show.

In preparation for the show, I had to wear a heart-rate variability monitor for three days, which recorded the times when I was on the go, stressed, and when I was resting. I had to keep a diary alongside it so that what I was doing matched up with the information recorded. I then had a session with Janine to discuss it all.

It was so incredible to see the results plainly in black and white – or rather red and green. Red on the graph represented 'on the go', with spikes of stress, and rest times were represented in green. The gold standard is not to spike too much and to be able to oscillate from red back to green with relative ease.

So, there was a spike of red in the morning as cortisol helped to get me from lying down to getting up, but I choose to take ten to twenty minutes to myself to meditate or do some breathwork, and while I know the theory that this is good for me and I have felt the benefits, it was great to see the swathe of green on the graph as I did it. Janine told me that this is a great way to train the body to go from red to green with ease, first thing in the morning when the systems are firing, give the message 'we rest now' (not the same as hitting snooze and going back to sleep, it has to be said – sorry). It sets the body up to be able to do that throughout the day.

The graph was red as I did normal things – cooked meals, drove in traffic, dropped off and collected the kids – and it spiked where I got a bit of road rage or let out a roar at one of said kids when we were going to be late but, on the whole, it was normal on-the-go stuff.

At that time, I was writing content for my first online course and there was a massive section of green as I sat at my laptop and typed. That was lovely to see and is called flow – 'flow' is a concept in positive psychology, describing a state of being fully immersed in an activity. If you love what you do or have a pastime you enjoy, chances are you experience this too. We hear so much negativity about the sedentary lifestyle and time at a desk, so it was rather life-affirming to see this was a restorative place for me.

I also had green when I went to get my nails done and dozed in front of a reality TV show – things I would have previously thought frivolous but when you see it amongst the on-the-go stuff, you begin to realise that we need to start thinking about ourselves in the same way as we think about our smartphones. We need to shut down all the apps and recharge the battery regularly.

The sleep part was even more interesting. Even though I was having a good chunk of quality green-coloured sleep for six or seven hours, my first hour or so before that was red. My heart-rate data showed that I was asleep, but I wasn't in restorative sleep as my mind was running over everything that had happened that day and what was to come tomorrow. Until I had this meeting with Janine and received this information, I 100 per cent thought that this was a perfect time for all this; as I turned out the light and finally lay in silence, I rather enjoyed a personal debrief of what had happened during the day and what things I had to do tomorrow. Sometimes, it was as simple as what I would wear the next day or what I needed to get for dinner but it was enough to wind me up so that I wasn't getting the adequate rest I needed.

The suggested antidote was to start writing a list at my desk as I finished work for the day, and before lights out, a brain dump of what was in my head. I will confess, I haven't been religious with this, it feels like more work, but I have become way more conscious of not letting my thoughts go there, instead I just focus on my breathing and I fall asleep. Another confession: I am typing this chapter at 10 p.m. on the laptop in bed, but this is a rare occurrence.

Since working with Janine, I have really become aware of my energy levels – how much I am giving out and where, as well as when and how I will replenish that energy rather than just assuming it is an infinite resource as I run myself into the ground. If I have a busy week at work, my weekend will be slower, I will look to book in something like a sauna and ice-bath or just chill out reading my book. I don't get it right all the time but I am getting better at looking at my diary and making sure where there is red, there will also be green.

Wearable tech

I don't wear any tech devices; maybe I'll change my mind here in time but, for now, I think they would make me obsess. I am my own wearable tech and judge my own energy levels and mood, matching it up to how I have been living – often the answers lie there. However, I was given great insight from the technology of The Wellbeing Advantage and I know that, for many, smart devices can be hugely beneficial. I would always start with tuning in to how I feel and with a caveat of not obsessing over numbers – let them inform you, not rule you or stress you out. Here is some advice on choosing the right tech for you.

1. **Identify your needs and goals**

   Are you focused on improving sleep, increasing physical activity, managing stress or tracking nutrition?

   Choose technology that complements your lifestyle and fits into your daily schedule.

2. **Research and evaluate**

   Opt for devices or apps that are easy to navigate and understand.

   Ensure the technology provides reliable and accurate data to track your progress and make informed decisions.

   Check if the technology integrates with other devices or platforms you use.

   Consider the initial purchase price, subscription fees and potential maintenance costs. Also consider the potential for long-term use and whether the technology will remain relevant as your needs evolve.

3. **Consider specific features**
   - Sleep tracking
   - Activity tracking
   - Heart-rate monitoring
   - Stress management

   Look for features like guided meditation or breathing exercises. It can be great to take part in challenges and log how many days in a row you show up – it can be a great motivator.

Check if your smartphone already has some of these features.
4. **Read reviews and seek recommendations**
   - Consult online reviews
   - Seek recommendations from friends or experts

   If possible, try out a device or app before committing to a long-term purchase.

Be careful where and from whom you are taking your health advice. Walking ten thousand steps a day came from a marketing company to sell a pedometer ahead of the 1964 Tokyo Olympics. Yes, increasing movement is good for us and walking is great, but do you need to glance at your watch at 10 p.m. when you're winding down on the couch, see you're at 9,000 and charge around the block several times until you hit the magic number? No, that is bonkers (Wedesweiler, 2023).

When it comes to your health, you are an expert on your own body. Know your normal, and turn to qualified medical professionals for health advice and before starting something new.

And remember: trying something and finding that it doesn't work for you isn't a failure, it's learning. I've been able to step away from food tracking and calorie-counting but I have tried both over the years and while ultimately I've evolved to see it as potentially harmful, there was certainly learning about nutrition, my eating habits and connecting what I was eating to how I felt that was all part of the process.

Have a think about rest and recharging in your life. Where do you think you could find your green? If it's not happening enough, start to book it in. For every fight-or-flight stress response, we need a rest and digest. The modern world means so many of us stay in our stress response as there are constant demands on us, and this chronic stress can impact on our health long term. Our systems need to have rest-and-digest time to function at their optimum, so do yourself a favour and switch off, restore yourself. *Slow down, wind down and rest. Find your green within the red.*

Forest bathing

You can literally find your green by heading to the trees. Forest bathing originated in Japan in the 1980s and involves engaging all of your senses – listening to the sounds, breathing in the smells, taking in the sights, and reaching out to touch the trees or plants around you. It means truly slowing down – when do we give ourselves time to do that?

Stress raises levels of the hormone cortisol. Long-term stress and chronic elevations in cortisol play a role in high blood pressure, heart disease, headaches and many other ailments. In test subjects, levels of cortisol decreased after a walk in the forest, compared with people who walked in a laboratory setting.

One Japanese study showed a rise in number and activity of immune cells called 'natural killer cells' – which fight viruses and cancer – among people who spent three days and two nights in a forest versus people who took an urban trip (Li & others, 2006). This benefit lasted for more than a month after the forest trip!

Remember to be as present as you can and go slowly – the aim is to wind down, not to burn calories. You can't charge through the forest bet into a crime podcast, that's for another day.

Medical professionals are getting on board with this too. Doctors in New Zealand were among the first to issue green prescriptions in the late 1990s, and it's become an established part of the government's health policy there (Patel & others, 2011).

Here in Ireland, GP Dr Mark Rowe has also begun issuing green prescriptions to patients with an entry pass to the gardens at Mount Congreve near his practice in County Waterford. I know because he told me himself as we went forest bathing there together. To be clear: there is no bath in forest bathing – clothes are on and you are bathing in all of the sounds and sights around you!

So, you don't have to be completely still to be at rest but you do need to slow down and allow your body to unwind.

Look at your week now and make a plan for where rest and wind-down will feature for you.

WELL? OVER TO YOU ...

Do you allow yourself to rest regularly?

Do you feel under pressure to be productive and 'doing' all the time?

What's your relationship with stress like? (Use a scale of 1 to 10 where 1 is 'rarely experience' and 10 is 'stressed all the time')

Do you struggle to fall asleep or stay asleep?

What do you do to reduce the stress in your life?

When do you feel most relaxed?

Which of the following do you – or could you – prioritise in your life to restore you?

- Time in nature
- A sea dip
- Meditation – guided or otherwise
- Breathwork – guided or otherwise
- Spa treatment – massage, nails, etc.
- Reading/Listening to an audiobook
- Guided mindfulness practice – there are some available on www.wouldyoubewell.ie
- Watching relaxing TV/film (violence, thrillers and scrolling at the same time doesn't count here)
- Spending time with your pet
- Taking a warm bath
- Listening to relaxing music
- Being present with people who light you up
- Spending time alone
- Journalling
- Stretching
- Yoga
- A hobby you love – crafting, art, etc.

Consider some of the ones you haven't tried but would like to. Build up a toolkit of restful techniques you can lean on a regular basis and turn to in times of major stress.

Choose one that you will prioritise this week.

List one new technique you would like to try.

SLEEP HYGIENE TIPS

Make your bedroom as dark and quiet as possible, using earplugs and an eye mask if necessary.
Make sure your bed and pillow are comfortable, and the room temperature is cool but not too cold.
Go to bed and wake up at the same time each day, even on weekends, to set a consistent circadian rhythm.
Limit caffeine and alcohol close to bedtime, as they are stimulants that disrupt sleep quality.
Avoid heavy, spicy or fatty meals before bed, as they can cause indigestion and discomfort.
Spend time in natural light, especially in the morning, to help regulate your body's sleep–wake cycle.

Exercise regularly but not too close to bedtime.
Create a relaxing bedtime routine – engage in calm, relaxing activities, such as reading a book, listening to soft music, meditating or taking a warm bath – to signal to your body that it's time to sleep.
While staying hydrated is important, limiting large amounts of liquid close to bedtime can help prevent night-time awakenings.

JUST BREATHE

At the time of writing, I have just finished my third level of breathwork teacher training with The Blissful Breath Academy, which means this is a perfect time to write this chapter. There are five levels of training in total and, all going well, I will be a breathwork master by the time this book is published.

When I think about what I want you to get out of this book, it's mainly a mindset shift. I hope you will feel empowered that wellness is something you can do, not a stick with which to beat yourself. As I've said, the path is going to look different to everybody as we are all unique, but if there was one tangible practice I would love you to take on board, it's breathwork.

It can be hard to understand the need to dedicate time to breathing – sure, we breathe all the time. As with many things, the inherent ways we are born with begin to slip away as life takes over, and breathing is one of them. If we begin to make space in our day to focus on and slow down our breathing, it can have a profound impact on our wellbeing.

Your breath is linked to so many systems in your body, but most notably your central nervous system, and regular breathwork can bring a sense of calm during your practice and after. It's also a way to dedicate time to just slowing down and being still – not something we manage to do very much, though it's something we all need.

If you struggle to get your head around mindfulness and meditation, breathwork is a great way to access many of the similar benefits but with something to focus on: your breath. Intentional breathing can take us from fight or flight to rest and digest.

I have trained with Níall Ó Murchú at his Blissful Breath Academy and it was Níall who introduced me to the power of breath. In the early days of my radio show, he was making a name for himself as a Wim Hof instructor, helping people into ice baths before it had become as mainstream as it is now. So, off I went with my recording equipment to have a chat with this madman who liked walking up snowy mountains in his shorts.

He and his wife Josie are two of the best people you will ever meet, which is probably down to all the deep breathing they do! I'm happy to say they have become friends over the years but back then they were just two friendly people, inviting me into their home. They have an incredible story to tell, as most people working in the wellness industry do. They had four children under the age of four, including twin girls, had suffered great bereavement and loss in their family, and were struggling to cope with it all when they happened upon breathwork and cold-water therapy. Starting small – a cold shower when the kids were down for the night and breathing deeply together – they found not only an ability to cope and enjoy life again, but this practice opened up new paths for them, which ultimately became their life and careers.

I recorded a little of Níall's story for the radio show and then it was time to get serious: I really was going to get into an ice bath in his back garden, it was only a matter of time. He explained to me that we were going to prepare our bodies by breathing, so I lay on his sitting-room floor and for the next fifteen minutes or so he directed me through a series of deep breaths and some breath holds with rests in between – it was like nothing I had ever experienced before. My whole body was tingling and I was completely in the moment, focusing on nothing but how I was feeling and my breath.

After the final round, Níall explained that he would leave me to change – I had the swim costume ready under my tracksuit – telling me I was to try and stay in this relaxed, almost hypnotic state. He would be outside the door and we would head to the garden but we wouldn't get into chit-chat, but just stay focused. And so I did. Out I went and there, at the bottom of the garden, was what reminded me of the big blue bottle bins you see in pubs or hotels, it was full to the brim with water and massive chunks of ice.

I think Níall might have had his bodhrán, which he was striking gently to keep the breathing going, while my mind was wondering how I was going to do it. I just kept breathing and walking towards the bath. I had been prepped that, when I stepped in, I would recoil in shock and my breath would quicken but that I was to focus on returning to the calming breath we had been working on. And I did it! It wasn't easy, especially at first – my whole body was screaming at me to get out and run, there was panic – but then I started to catch my breath, to breathe a little more deeply, and a calmness began to come through the chaos.

Unbelievably, I was able to sink down into the bath until it covered my shoulders and smile for a quick photo with the massive ice chunks bobbing around me. I didn't stay in for too long, but I did it! That was my first introduction to the power of the breath, to calm us and centre us in the most challenging of situations.

There has also been an explosion of outdoor saunas and ice baths up and down the country and it's amazing to see how mainstream it has become but, back then, it was niche for sure, even though it's harking back to practices our ancestors leaned on all the time.

James Nestor in his 2020 book *Breath: The New Science of a Lost Art* explores how 68–90 per cent of people are not breathing as efficiently as they could be, and that this is having an impact on their health. Coupled with the stresses we looked at in the last chapter, we are often in a constant state of fight or flight, with our nervous system on high alert, without us even knowing it.

Making time to focus on your breath is an incredible way to bring you back to the present moment, to bring you back to rest and digest, to feel calm, to respond rather than to react, and to ensure your body's systems are functioning as they should. Your body is always trying to get back to homeostasis, a sense of balance, and your breathing can help bring that about.

Three deep breaths will tell your nervous system that you are safe. If there was imminent danger, there would be no time for that, so by slowing everything down, starting with your breath, you let your body's systems know that all is well. You also feel more in control of what you do next. If I have a presentation to give or I'm live on air for a show that I've never done before, I will always take three calming breaths with a focus on a long, slow exhale. It doesn't eradicate nerves completely but I feel more in control and calmer for sure. Short breaths, taken high up in our chest, can elevate our heart rate and bring about a panicked feeling, whereas a deep breath with a long, slow exhale does the very opposite.

If you find it challenging to sit and meditate or to bring mindfulness into your life, breathwork can give you something to focus on. When you breathe like this you are mindful, you are in the present moment and you can get yourself to a meditative state.

Even two minutes is like a reset for your brain. Breathing can wind us down and help us sleep, and it can help you start the day with calm, setting the tone for what's to come.

I have tried so many practices, and there is something about breathwork that has really captured me. On the weekends when we learn and gain our qualification as breathwork instructors, the feeling among the group is incredible, I've never experienced anything like it. Doing copious amounts of breathing together, oxytocin is released, and the sense of calm and camaraderie is honestly quite mind-blowing.

I've met people on the course who have had all kinds of tough circumstances thrown their way in life, and embracing breathwork has helped them so much that they were empowered to learn more. I haven't had some of those losses, but I did arrive to the first session of the weekend frazzled after a long week with stresses of my own, visiting my pal in hospital after her mastectomy and interviewing a beautifully brave advocate for consent who had waived her anonymity to bring her attacker to court. I hadn't slept well all week, we were house-hunting and mortgage-seeking, and with all the other plates spinning, I was wound up.

I was wound down by the first evening's breathwork session. I slept beautifully that night and floated out of that hotel on the Sunday – breathing slowly can change you.

Since then, I have committed ten minutes every day to coherent breathing (in for a count of four and out for a count of four) and I feel the difference. I can't be out there at that hotel with Níall and Josie every weekend (more is the pity), but I can bring a piece of that experience into my everyday life. That is the wellness key – how can you integrate the practices that work for you and weave them into how you live so that they become who you are.

> Check out my guided breathwork sessions on
> www.wouldyoubewell.ie

Part 3
SOUL

I hope you have taken a deeper dive into your mind and body in the previous two sections but I'm sure you were already aware of the concepts of physical and mental health. However, you might never have considered your spiritual health and the role your soul plays in your wellbeing.

Think of your soul as your essence – what makes you, you. What lights you up.

We often attribute so much of who we are to what we do, whether that be our job title or the labels we have, such as parent, sibling, partner or friend. While your life experiences and your people help shape you, who are you at your core? What gives you meaning and purpose?

Where in your life do you devote time to this or reflect on what it means to you? If your soul is the essence of who you are, then a focus here is essentially a coming back to who you are. We can get pulled away by life but it's good for our wellbeing when we make time to find our way back.

This will mean something different to everyone; what it means and how you get there will be very personal and as unique as you are. Cut through the overwhelm to find what works for you.

In this section, we will look at the key aspects of spiritual wellbeing, the common misconceptions and the surprising ways you can connect to your soul.

The key aspects of spiritual wellbeing are:
- Meaning and purpose
- Values and beliefs
- Inner harmony – being at peace with who you are
- Connection
- Personal growth.

All of these come back to knowing who you are at your core. There are so many reasons we can move away from ourselves, our busy lives, our responsibilities, our life experiences – we can spend so much time looking out that we forget to connect back in. Distraction and busyness can let time fly by and suddenly you wonder, 'What happened to me? Where did I go?'

The truth is, you're still here, you haven't gone anywhere. It can be tricky to answer the questions 'Who am I?' and 'What do I really want?', which seems bonkers when we live with ourselves 100 per cent of the time.

As we move through the chapters in this section, let them be a reminder of the importance of letting go of who you think you should be and empower you to be who you really are.

When you know who you are, you know what you need and when you are connected to yourself, you can speak up and out for others too. That sense of community and being connected to something greater is just as important as the connection to yourself. I consider it the magic fairy dust of life.

When you answer the question 'Who am I?' do you immediately go to what you do for a living? Do you answer with who you are to other people – wife, husband, partner, mother, father, brother, sister, friend? What you do for a living, what you're studying or who you are caring for is very much a part of your life, but is it truly who you are? It's an abstract question and it's not an easy answer but it just takes some thought. What lights you up in life? What are your values? What are the things in life that you gravitate towards?

This is the you that only you really know. You can show parts of it to people, but it is here where your deepest desires, dreams, fears and memories live. Connecting here is a massive component of your wellbeing.

MEANING AND PURPOSE

Living a life of meaning and purpose is woven into the fabric of wellbeing. It can also reek a little of privilege; I often think of people struggling to make ends meet or facing a major life trauma and to ask them to consider a life with purpose seems almost patronising. There is no right or wrong, but finding it in your life can lead to greater wellbeing and fulfilment. Research suggests that having a sense of purpose is linked to better health and longevity (Mehta, 2025).

So, where do we find meaning (feeling significant) and purpose (expression of meaning)? We derive meaning and purpose from our social networks, our families, our values, our cultures, our work and our environments. It's not the same as happiness, which can be fleeting and experience-based. It's not the same as material possession, it's an intrinsic feeling of contentment that you are living your life as best you can. You can find it at home with your family or speaking out for others; only you will know what is right for you.

Ask yourself the following questions:
- What do I truly care about?
- What are my values?
- What are my character strengths?

There are exercises for strengths and values in the back of the book. Identifying these can help you find more meaning and purpose in your life.

Being kind and being of service is linked to greater levels of meaning and purpose in life. This can be something like volunteering but it can also be in a caring role for a family member or calling in on a neighbour.

We often attribute success to material gain but so many people with financial success lack meaning in their lives. The mentality of striving for more can leave us feeling dissatisfied or that we never quite reach our destination. That feeling of disease can erode our sense of wellbeing.

SPEAK UP

There are people in our lives with whom we can be our true selves – our families, our best friends and our partners – but there can be parts that we hold back here too. Behaving in a way that is expected of us causes a strain. We can start to mask who we truly are.

To feel seen and heard is one of our basic human needs.

In the 1950s, American psychologist Abraham Maslow designed a theory of human motivation in which he outlined what a human needs, not just to survive but to thrive. It's often shown in a pyramid or in steps; you need to have your baseline needs met before you can move on to the next step. Then, when all those needs are being met, you can reach the point of 'self-actualisation', which means becoming the best version of yourself.

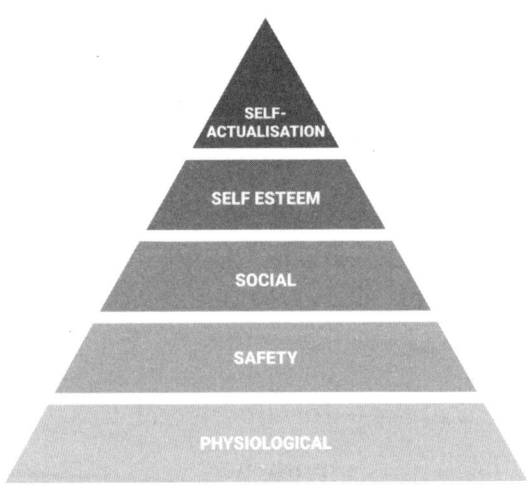

Figure 4: Maslow's Hierarchy of Needs

That middle, social section is the one we are talking about here. Feeling like you can be yourself and have people in your circle to do that with. This requires using your voice.

While you will have certain ways of behaving in a work setting or when meeting someone for the first time, it's important that you feel grounded enough in yourself to speak up when something isn't okay for you. So often in the places you find yourself, you can mould yourself to fit in, you can live a life that perhaps others wanted for you and, before you know it, you aren't living true to yourself.

There are so many of us who take on caring roles for ageing parents, run family businesses, take on college courses that were expected of us, fall into behaviours that we saw growing up that just became who we are. It can be easy to sleepwalk through the template of school, college, work, relationship, house and family. At what point do you ask yourself, 'What do I truly want?'

If you know how you feel, you know what you need, and when you know what you need you can ask for it. This isn't Veruca Salt demanding the golden-ticket vibes, this is you having your needs met and the only way for that to happen is to speak up.

First you need to speak to yourself and ask questions like:

- What do I need in this moment?
- Why is this bothering me?
- What is this bringing up for me?
- What would make this situation better?

When you have the answers, only you can work out what you are going to do next. There is no magic wand, we have to be our own fairy godmother and bring about these changes ourselves.

This might mean having conversations with your partner, your boss, your work colleague, your friends, your family. The tone will be important here; this isn't about moaning and nagging, this is taking down the mask and stating how you really feel. Scary, isn't it? It's also empowering. It can be good in these conversations to start your sentences with 'I ...' rather than 'You ...' So, 'I need more support with this project/the kids/caring for our parents, can we find a way together' vs 'You never help me ...'

Not speaking up for yourself will have an impact on your wellbeing if every time you hear a whisper from within that you need something or want change, you squash it down and ignore it. You might find yourself reaching for unhealthier foods and behaviours to comfort yourself because your needs are not being met, so you find another way to soothe yourself in the short term.

When I was studying to become an integrative health coach, looking at lifestyle and the impact it has on our wellbeing, it was repeated over and over that people know what they need, even if they are not sure how to get there. As a coach, you are there to hold space for them, asking some gentle questions, while they figure it out. We all know deep inside what we need, we have to block out the noise and listen to ourselves.

Did you know that women are statistically more likely to be diagnosed with an autoimmune disease than men? One of the reasons cited is that they often put the needs of others before their own. So, whatever your gender, whatever your setup, be aware that every time you deny yourself the opportunity to be heard, if it's causing you stress on a long-term basis, it is having an impact on your health.

When we speak up, does it mean that everything will magically go the way we want it to? Sadly, no. It's not possible for us to control the actions of others. Your siblings aren't going to instantly begin helping with your ageing parents, your boss isn't going to suddenly stop giving you high-pressure targets, your kids aren't going to stop needing you and some of your friends might still plan stuff without you. Remember, most of these people whose actions are causing you stress are not aware of the impact on you of their actions – it is unintentional, and they have their own stuff going on. Your boss is getting it from her boss or has financial and staffing pressures of her own, your siblings are leaving all the parent-caring to you because they aren't coping with their own situation, and your friends, like you, are overwhelmed with life and WhatsApp groups and it didn't even occur to them that you might fancy a walk on the beach too.

Perhaps your speaking up isn't a conversation, it's an action – Who else can help mind your parents? Is it time to look for another job? Why don't you be the one to suggest a walk on the beach with your friends?

And, always, you need to focus on the one thing you can control, which is you. Do you need to stay stuck in this stress loop, giving your energy to the actions of others? There are going to be times in your life when you will have to just accept people for who they are and mind your own energy.

I have a friend who became the sole carer for her ageing parents. There were all kinds of stresses involved, such as organising a nursing home, hospital visits, financial issues, as well as the demands of things like cleaning, shopping and spending time with her parents, and the emotional toll it was taking to see them this way. She also had a very busy job and a young family. Her two brothers, though lovely, were very little help. They both lived in different parts of the country and had other stuff going on. They would come down the odd weekend but, essentially, my friend knew, she was on her own in this. She had some tough days but, ultimately, she had to accept the situation and her brothers for who they were and be there for her parents at that time.

She spoke to her boss and took some compassionate leave to deal with all that her parents needed, to be there for her family and to focus on her mental health. She was very open with her husband about how she was struggling, so he was on board as a support system. She got back into walking, took a weekly yoga class, joined in on online wellness events and really took the time to mind herself. Did her situation change? Not really, but her attitude within it did. She spoke up for herself and made changes that made a big difference.

Having uncomfortable conversations and putting up boundaries is not easy to do. We don't like to raise our hand and ask for help, we think it makes us seem weak, that we are not coping when everyone else is. Guess what? Most people are struggling with something. Most people, if not all people, would appreciate more help and support in their lives. And when you ask for it, you give other people permission to speak up for themselves.

I do lots of work on a voluntary basis. I align myself with some charities, and I'm happy to help out if they want me to MC or give a talk without charge. As well as giving back it's also good for me to practise a new talk, a new workshop or just get my name out there a bit more, so I'm happy to do it and I think it's important. I also need to be careful that I don't do this too much and I value my own time and energy, so it's a balancing act.

I took part in a big wellness event one year. It was in another county, so the drive was substantial, and it meant that for what was a forty-five-minute talk, I was gone for most of a Sunday. I spend my weekdays running from one thing to the next, often asking my kids to hang on for a second while I finish something, so I like the weekends to be more about them and I also like to rest and recharge. So, I went to this event, I had a lovely time – I got to take part in a cacao and breathwork session and gave a short talk and met lovely people – and then drove home listening to some podcasts, all good.

However, when they asked me back the following year, I said I'd rather not. I wished them all the best and thanked them for asking me but said I'd already committed to a number of free gigs and I wouldn't be able to take this one on too, which was true. They offered me a fee, which was really kind, but I said, because of the distance and other things I had going on, I would decline, in order to be at home with my kids and to chill out. This was all over voice notes as things often are these days and

I'll never forget the voice note that came back from one of the organisers. She thanked me for my honesty and vowed to take a leaf out of my book. She was also juggling a million things and realised she was saying 'yes' to too much. I had felt quite guilty saying 'no', even though I knew in my gut it was right for me, but she was grateful and quite inspired by my no. Speaking up for yourself can be powerful, it can give people permission to do the same.

I recently got chatting to someone who was walking away from a relationship because the person they loved was in addiction. Having lost their sister to addiction and coming so far, they knew they couldn't do it again, especially when their partner wasn't ready to face the reality of seeking help. Uprooting your home and leaving someone you love is by no means an easy thing to do but ignoring the whispers of your own soul is worse. When you open up the channel of communication with yourself and you know what you need, you cannot let yourself down.

Speak up for your health

You are an expert on not only your own mind but your own body. When it comes to health issues, speak up and speak out. It can be tricky in any situation when we feel like the consumer coming to an expert, but if you have a feeling that something isn't right, that is enough of a symptom to get checked. If you don't feel you are getting the answers you need, it's time to find another practitioner. We don't want to get to a stage where we live in constant fear of illness and are continually getting checked just to get ahead of it, but if you feel unwell or that something has changed, you need to advocate for yourself. If you have a diagnosis and you don't feel you understand your treatment plan, ask again.

The average wait time for diagnosis for endometriosis is nine years. Women presenting with period pains that are impacting on their quality of life, spending several days in bed every month, which stops them from getting an education, going to work, socialising and is affecting their relationships, are often told that this is just a part of womanhood and are sent away. Not enough is known about the condition because women's health in particular is under-resourced, underfunded and often misdiagnosed.

Speak up for others

When you are using your voice for yourself, you can use it for others too; something that is needed more than ever in the world we live in. With the events of the past few years – inequality, division, war, corruption – we have begun to see that progress is not guaranteed.

It can be challenging to feel like our small voices can make a difference when it comes to such things, but all the small voices together really do make change. A shared post, a signed petition, a peaceful protest, an email to our leaders – they show our humanity and that we care. We need to be in the whole of our own health to be able to show up for those less fortunate, be they in our own communities or our global one.

I have interviewed many thought leaders and often asked how we are supposed to navigate this world but also help. They all said that we need to protect our own energy, build our own light so we can be a beacon for others. We can only shine our light brightly when we are strong within ourselves, physically, mentally and emotionally. For that, we need to speak up for our needs so that we can then use our voices to speak up for others who really need us.

I am a massive advocate for social change. So much can come from grassroots, people coming together to push from the bottom up for better. Scientists have found that when just 10 per cent of the population holds an unshakable belief, that belief will always be adopted by the majority of the society. This shows that even a small number can make a massive difference (www.sciencedaily.com).

In order to speak up for others, we need to have our solid foundation, we need to have advocated for ourselves and then we can bring that power elsewhere. Every struggle fosters resilience and empathy; kindness to ourselves breeds kindness to others.

DOING THINGS YOU THINK YOU CAN'T

A great way to find who we are and what lights us up is by taking a leap.

'We can do hard things.' The wonderful words written by Glennon Doyle in her 2020 book *Untamed*, which stayed with me long after I read the last page. We really can do hard things. We spoke about the growth and learning that comes in the struggle when we looked at our comfort zone. There is also much to be gained by doing something you think you can't.

A great place to start is the cold shower. I know, I can feel your resistance already, unless you are in the know and are glowing in your smugness. To turn your shower to cold, even for a few seconds until you catch your breath, can be transformative and serve as a template for all kinds of challenges that can come your way. You stand under the warm stream, everything in you dreading the cold, then finally turn down the dial and the shock hits you. You are now thrown into discomfort. Your breath starts to quicken as your body says no but you can calm this chaos. You can catch your breath, breathe a little deeper and while you aren't necessarily loving the cold water, you feel yourself relax. You are done, you can turn the water back up if you wish but, more often than not, you will emerge from that shower, victorious – you did it! You did something you thought you couldn't, and your body and mind will record the experience to call it up the next time you're faced with a similar dread.

For my fortieth birthday, my husband and I travelled to London for motivational speaker Tony Robbins' 'Unleash the Power Within' event. On the first day, we headed off to the Excel Arena, unsure of what to expect. There were 10,000 people queueing to get in when we arrived, they had come from all over the world to be there. We got chatting to people in line about what had brought them there and what they hoped to gain, until eventually we sat down, ready.

Out came Tony Robbins and, from the start, it's a high-energy performance and you are fully involved. While you have a workbook and there is some lecture and note-taking, you are also encouraged – no, expected – to bounce around the auditorium at many intervals throughout the day to booming music and flashing lights. There are highs and lows, and you are encouraged to delve deep in to your emotions and break out into groups with people you didn't come with. It's one hell of a ride.

It began on a Friday evening with an introduction to how it would all go down, the intel on Tony's voice, and then it was in with a bang. We would be walking on fire that night. He wanted us to start the whole experience with the imprint that we could do anything we put our minds to, front and centre. It was a long process to get to the fire pits, I can't even remember it all but it felt like we were being put in a hypnotic state. We were being brought to the highest highs where we believed we were champions, capable of all, and then he would reel us back in with health-and-safety warnings of the serious dangers involved and how best to navigate them. It was a lot. I can't even tell you how long that went on for, but it felt like a long time and then we were ready. We had begun chanting 'Yes, yes, yes' over and over, believing we could walk on fire and we were to keep up this chant as we headed out to the car park and the fire pits.

My husband is one of the most amiable people you will ever meet, you can literally bring him anywhere and he will settle in. He was up for all of it – the bouncing around, the shouting at our self-limiting beliefs, the chatting to everyone around us – and he was now taking to this fire-walking chat like a duck to water, whereas I was having some serious doubts. We had been warned, several times from the podium, of the potential danger, of being burned and what safety measures were in place. We were told that when we got to the other side of the fire pit, we must put all celebration on hold until we were hosed down by a waiting staff member. I was scared. I was chanting 'yes' but my head was saying 'no', asking what the hell I thought I was doing. As we spilled out into the night, I could see the moon in the sky and up ahead a series of fire pits and the thousands of people beginning to form mini queues in front of them.

We got to what would be our line. It's all a bit hazy, which is what leads me to think we were in a trance of sorts, but I just kept inching forward. I became aware that my husband had breezed over but even as I try to recall that memory now I can't see him do it, I'm not sure if he ended up a couple of people ahead. It came to my turn; I could see the pit of hot coals out in front of me, there were metal containers of the stuff alongside it and masked men with shovels manning each one. I'm sure the masks were to protect them from the smoke but they looked sinister. My fear was still palpable although my chanting continued.

Just as I got to the top of the queue, a woman stood in front of me, blocking me from the pit. I remember this part clearly. I thought, *They know I'm scared*, but she just held my gaze and was now leading us in the 'yes, yes, yes'. I was saying the words but was starting to freak out inside as I watched one of the masked men shovel fresh hot coals onto my path. I can see the woman now; she looked me dead in the eyes and said, 'You've got this.' Next thing I know, I'm over the other side and my husband is hugging me. We did it.

That high, as we walked back into the auditorium, unscathed, is one of the biggest in my life. I would in many ways call it a spiritual experience – a deep connection to myself, to the people around me and to a bit of magic I can't quite put my finger on.

Years later, I was in Derry with a film crew for *Ireland AM* and one of the segments involved me skateboarding around the city. When we arrived to meet my skateboard instructor, we were behind in our filming schedule and I only had thirty minutes to go from zero to hero. I had no previous experience skateboarding and my guide was a little shocked, saying he would usually have at least a couple of hours but as the drizzle began to make the paths more treacherous, he taught me as best he could.

Dressed in my knee and arm pads and helmet, looking distinctively uncool, it was time to head to the Peace Bridge – it's a fairly modern bridge, built after the Good Friday Agreement, and made of sheets of corrugated metal. It curves as it meets the path and so I was expected to cruise along this bridge on my skateboard and glide past the cameraman and into the pathway that was populated with people. I took off along to the halfway mark of the bridge wondering how I got there, completely and utterly terrified. There were families and couples strolling along and I feared for their lives and mine. Then, suddenly, it came to me: I can do this, I walked on fire. This is where the power lies – the more you do what you think you can't, the more you begin to believe that you can do anything that you put your mind to.

You are more open to the opportunities around you and sometimes, even a little magic. You don't need a fire pit or a skateboard, I bet there are lots of times you have done very hard things, you just haven't given yourself credit. Maybe you overcame adversity, gave birth, set up a business, supported a loved one – it's in these experiences that we can learn who we truly are.

WELL? OVER TO YOU …

Think about your life achievements to date and write down a number of them – learning to walk, to read, to talk, any other languages you might speak, getting through school, getting your first job, opening a bank account, getting married, having a baby, taking care of a baby, opening a business, buying or renting a home – go deep with whatever your timeline of achievements is.

Now, think back on each one and how daunting and new each one was – although many were exciting. Each step took effort and work, there were obstacles and challenges but you did it. Often, we forget to see how far we have come and how much we have learnt.

What's one of the biggest challenges you have overcome in your life? Remember, just getting through something isn't easy and should be considered a success.

What parts of your personality helped you?

If you could approach any of your life challenges again, would you do anything differently?

What has each challenge and achievement taught you about yourself?

When do you feel the most empowered or proud of yourself? (I hope it's right now looking at that list.)

SAGE THE ROOM

Spirituality is having a moment. It's always been around but it's become rather trendy. We're awash with sage, cacao and crystals – things that were once niche have now become mainstream.

The move away from organised religion has long fascinated me, particularly here in Ireland. We have a long history as a Catholic country with a close connection between religion, state and education, but this history has been marred by controversies of corruption and abuse that went all the way to the Vatican. The hurt and pain felt through generations here has in no small way contributed to the dwindling numbers of people attending mass every Sunday.

I was raised a Catholic, as were both my parents. I was christened, made my Communion and Confirmation and went to a Catholic school. We went to mass every Sunday (though I stopped in my teens). I wasn't mad on the idea, but the place would be packed and every other family in our area would be there too. You could have a nose at the guy you fancied, standing there with his parents in a pew. We would come back in the front door to smell the roast beef that had been cooking while we prayed – all very wholesome and traditional.

I did complain a couple of times about having to go, about not wanting to wear my 'good' coat and shoes (the guy I fancied was going to be there!), but my dad said something that has stayed with me. He understood that I found it boring but I should try to look on it as a chance to reflect on the week gone by – was there anything I might like to have handled differently, anything that went well, and then look to the week ahead. A moment to just pause and take stock while enjoying the music and the calm setting. Now, it took me years to fully appreciate what he said but there is something in it for sure. While I have since taken matters into my own hands and mass is not a part of our every week, I do still recognise that there needs to be a place in my week to pause and reflect.

As humans, we crave that feeling of belonging, to feel a part of something. Ritual, ceremony and community are all mainstays in our sense of wellbeing, and this was once provided by the Church. There are still plenty of people who have great faith and I fully respect that, just as I do those who are not religious at all. I don't believe that in order to be a good person you need to follow a religious faith. However, I have begun to wonder if we have thrown away the spirituality baby with the religion bathwater. What are we replacing it with?

Spirituality can mean different things to different people; it can have overlap into religion and people can find their spirituality there, but the two can also be mutually exclusive. For some people, spirituality can be their connection to nature, the way a walk in the forest makes them feel, that feeling by the sea or with the changing seasons. For others, it's the sense that there is something bigger than just us, a sense of awe and wonder – you can feel it within humanity or an incredible view.

A few years back, Emily, a great friend of mine, told me that she was heading to a full-moon circle on a beach not far from my house and asked if I fancied going along. She told me to bring my yoga mat and all she really knew was that there would be some chanting and that we would get into the sea, but apart from that she wasn't certain.

Chanting makes me a little bit uncomfortable but I was intrigued, and I'm up for most experiences anyway. We met in the car park and trudged our mats up the pathway towards the dunes. Now, I was thinking that this was a fairly niche experience; I was expecting to see about ten or twenty people – I kid you not, it was like a festival when we got there. There were at least a couple of hundred people, all lined up on their mats, lots of them had little fairy lights strewn around them for when the sun set and they were all snuggled up in blankets, ready. Patrick, the guy hosting the event, was in the middle by a roaring fire and he was chatting to and hugging people as they settled in.

When we got started, he led us in some breathwork, and as we were breathing deeply, he was shouting uplifting words encouraging us to believe in ourselves. We all then headed down to the sea and, as the moon rose before our very eyes, we got in for a moonlit dip. Some groups were holding hands and standing in a circle; there was lots of mingling, with strangers becoming friends, and the whole atmosphere was euphoric.

I got chatting to different people and groups and we laughed together before enjoying hot drinks back up in the dunes. People could stay for as long as they wanted. I went to a good few of these meet-ups, which still go on, although they've moved from the dunes to protect them, and I also invited Patrick the organiser on to my radio show. He told me in our chat that many, many people have come up to him either at the event or contacted him online to say that these meet-ups have literally saved their lives. They had found themselves at a low ebb mentally and coming together to breathe, to connect and to feel seen, had been a catalyst to them feeling better.

I feel like I always had a lean towards the spiritual. A friend of mine always had a pack of angel cards in her house and I loved to pick one. It's like reading the horoscope in a way, isn't it? You wouldn't want to plan your entire life around them but being open to a message or a learning from one is something I remember sparking something in me. I now start and end my day by lighting a candle. It's a very small act but it's that moment to pause and reflect. It sets a tone, an intention. In the morning, I light it before a quick meditation or breathwork session – usually ten minutes – and, in the evening, it marks the transition from the day into wind-down mode. Both times, the candle sets the tone and I've become obsessed with the various scents.

Not everyone is ready to embrace the spiritual. A few weeks after my dad died, I had dinner with a group of friends. We did a Kris Kindle and one friend made sure I got her gift as she said it would be a good thing for me to do. It was my first smudge kit, which is basically a collection of things to enable you to 'smudge' or 'cleanse' your home, and included sage, palo santo and a feather. The sage and palo santo are burned and then when you waft the smoke about with the feather, it either resets the energy or brings a more positive energy. I'm not sure these things have been measured in a science lab, but there is an intention set.

I arrived home from my evening and everyone was in bed. I sat with a glass of wine and decided that there was no time like the present to get banishing any unnecessary negativity. So, I got the sage going and began wafting it into the corners of every room with my large turquoise feather. My journey continued up the stairs. I didn't head into the kids' rooms as you never wake a sleeping child, but I decided the room I shared with my husband was fair game. As he slept, I wafted that sage around the bedroom, with a good few blasts above his head for good measure, and then I headed back downstairs. I opened the windows and envisaged the negativity flowing out and a new start for me and my grief. I settled back down onto the couch to finish my wine, delighted with myself and my fortuitous Kris Kindle gift.

A while later, it was time for bed and I climbed in, ready for sleep. As I closed my eyes, my husband jumped up out of the bed to say he couldn't sleep, he had whatever I had been spraying right up his nose and if I were ever to attempt to do it again, he would leave. And leave he did, to the spare room (which I had actually saged, too, but perhaps not as intensely), and I was left alone. We laugh about it now, we did the next morning, and I get how irritating it must have been. I'm not sure I'd have taken kindly to it either, but it just goes to show that there are different spirituality strokes for different folks.

We both now favour the palo santo, which is a less pungent smell, and will waft that around from time to time. I often say it to the kids when they are sharing a worry that, when we have talked it through, we will get the scent going and the intention is set, to move that energy on. Do I think a piece of scented wood will replace a therapist or a GP? No, but it's another piece of the puzzle.

The Celtic Wheel

This is a return to ancient practice. The Celtic Wheel represents the calendar our Celtic ancestors used to mark out the year in seasons and festivals. I first heard about it in relation to our wellbeing during a workshop with yoga teacher Sarah Shannon and went on to do an online course with her too. From the excitement of spring, full of energy and new ideas, to going within in winter to rest and recharge. The Celtic calendar also suggests that January is resting and dreaming, imagining what's to come with a gentle energy. I'm all for it. No need to go full throttle with the restrictive resolutions. The festival we are

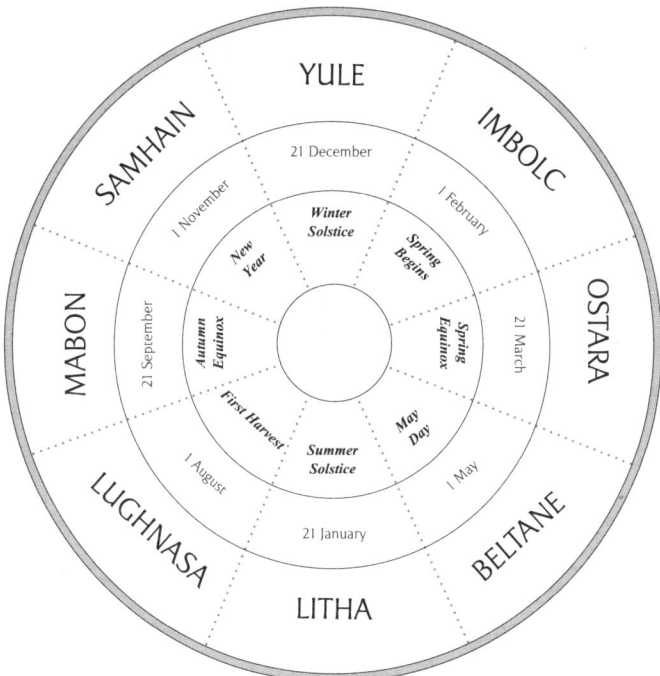

Figure 5: The Celtic calendar

probably most familiar with in Ireland is Samhain, the harvest time at the end of the summer, a chance to celebrate all the work that has gone into the year and to take stock.

All of these things represent spirituality to me and I dip in and out of each. There are no hard and fast rules, rather a weaving into my everyday. I sit with a cup of cacao on occasion with a focus on heart opening; you can do it with a cup of tea, the ingredients aren't the same but the intention can be.

The ritual of bedtime, from the candle, to the dimmed lighting, to the lavender oil. The body responds and begins to wind down. It's a chance to be grateful for the smallest of things that day. These are the little ways I weave spirituality into my everyday.

For me, it's about looking at where you can bring ritual, reflection and community to your life. In the trees, by the sea, under the sun, moon and stars, and in your home. It's using this for a moment of reflection to pause and to feel a sense of something outside of yourself. Find what works for you.

NATURE

Nature is a great way to connect to our soul; we are, after all, nature ourselves. When we are in nature, we can often feel as if we are connecting to something that is greater than we are – the wind in the forest trees, the waves crashing to the shore, the swell of the ocean or the sun rising. We need to get out into nature for our mental, physical and spiritual health. Research suggests that spending at least two hours per week in nature is associated with improved mental health and wellbeing. While this is the minimum, we can break it down into shorter periods, like fifteen minutes a day. Or even a microbreak, such as taking your shoes off to stand on the grass or just have a cuppa outside, can offer mood-boosting and focus-enhancing benefits.

I love to watch a sunrise or sunset, so worth the trip if you have a decent viewing spot close by. The early-morning alarm call can sting at first, but watching the sun come up is like pure magic and you get such a sense of anything being possible as you watch the new day dawn.

A dip in the sea is another cracker. Cold as it can be, it is an all-encompassing whack of nature – the cold brings you into the present moment and you are literally in nature. I'm a head dunker for the full reset, and I'm always filled with a sense of gratitude for how it makes me feel to be bobbing about in the water, taking in the view around me.

You don't have to get in to get the benefits – even looking at the sea, listening to the waves and walking along the shore is a dose of nature. Kids are all over this, they constantly kick off their shoes to feel the grass, the sand and to paddle in the waves. I've been guilty of pulling my kids back so they don't get wet or mucky; let's stop doing that and let's get wet and mucky too – it's good for us.

Wonder and awe plays an important role in our spiritual wellbeing. The personal definition of awe can be challenging to put your finger on, but it's described in the dictionary as a 'feeling of great respect, usually mixed with fear or surprise'. We can often feel awe when we are taking in a view or having a particular experience like a lake swim, watching a waterfall or standing on the top of a mountain, and it can be good to feel rather insignificant as you stand alongside a vast ocean or forest or look into the night sky and the universe above.

Mooning

More on the full-moon ritual. Don't panic, there is no one sacrificed, my husband remains unharmed in this endeavour – in fact, he often joins in and my daughter is a fan too. Because the moon has a cycle, much like women and the tides, it gives us an opportunity to start again. When the moon is full, I have a think about what I might like to let go of, things that aren't serving me anymore. I write these things down on a piece of paper and then burn the paper; the new-moon cycle begins the next day and it's a fresh start. Now, there are months that can go by and I miss the bloody thing, but when I notice a big, juicy moon in the sky – I notice the moon a lot – I just take a moment to stop and think about what I need to let go of.

Even without the writing and burning, it's a good idea to get your eyes up to the sky. There is a lookout close to where we live and we will often go, slot a coin into the telescope and see the moon up close; along with sunrise and sunset, it's a gorgeous bit of nature to connect with.

Using the cycles of nature and leaning into them, such as the letting go as the full moon turns to new or getting cosy through the winter months and wintering until spring, can be a positive thing to do.

Tree hugging

Trees are a borderline obsession of mine, I love them. We need them for our survival; we hear so much now about global warming and climate change, and it's utterly terrifying. Planting more trees and not chopping down so many of the beautiful ones we have now would have a massive impact on CO_2 levels.

One of my favourite books is *To Speak for the Trees* by Diana Beresford-Kroeger, an amazing woman who is a world-renowned botanist and medical biochemist. In her book, published in 2019, she speaks of the merit of trees and of her life being raised within the Celtic tradition by her family members in Lisheen Valley in the south of Ireland where she spent her summers. Nature is key to the Celtic way of life, and it was whilst she was in Lisheen that she learned the word *mothaitheacht* used to describe the recognition of trees as sentient beings. The Celts believed that some people could feel this more than others and it's described as a feeling in your upper chest of energy and sound passing through you.

I think I have that, or I'm just mad about trees. A walk in the woods, watching them sway in the wind, seeing the buds come on the bare branches in spring and the flowering blossoms and magnolias send me into overdrive. I have one pal who shares this love and we send each other photos of what we call 'tree porn' and cat videos. We are still great craic on a night out, I swear, but these photos and videos always bring a smile to my face.

Finding a connection to nature can be personal and unique for you, but the themes are universal. Whether it's growing a herb garden or a veg patch or making a date for a walk in the park or a picnic on the beach, to be in nature is to stir your soul, revive your senses and boost your wellbeing.

LIVING YOUR BEST LIFE

What would it look like to live your best life?

Think about it. Close your eyes and imagine you and your best life. What are you doing? Who are you with? Who are you? Is it close or far away from where you are now? Sometimes, we automatically think about material things, for example financial freedom that, of course, would have some positives – but is that truly life at its best?

I had an experience once that gave me a sharp shock of what life is all about. My husband and I were lucky enough to get tickets to see U2 in Paris on the weekend of his birthday. My mother-in-law moved in to mind the kids and two new kittens, and off we went. We had friends flying in to join us for the concert but for the first day and night we were on our own and we loved it. We were crossing roads holding hands without having to be on high alert with two toddlers – it was absolute bliss. We did a bit of shopping and strolled along without a care in the world. We walked up a street at the back of one of the most expensive department stores with designer labels taking up every window. There was a Porsche parked outside and the boot was open and several large bags were being placed inside. We looked over, thinking, *Wow, imagine that life.*

We headed out for dinner that night and then back to the hotel. I was conscious that the next night would be a big one, and as there was an Ireland football game on the television that evening, we settled in for the night. My phone started to ping with messages from people asking if we were okay following the explosion. At first, I was answering back with jokey texts about the shopping and my credit card, but the messages were coming through so much that we turned to the news channel to see that there had been a terrorist attack at a concert venue close by. This is not a woe-is-me tale; we were lucky, safe in our hotel while people lost their lives and were seriously injured, but the fear still made it into our room.

We watched as François Hollande, the president of France at the time, declared a state of emergency, closing the airports and borders until further notice. I didn't really sleep that night, unsure of what would happen next. The incident had been isolated and dealt with, and I dread to think what the reality of that was like for everyone involved. It was such a relief to walk out of our hotel the next morning and see buses going by and normal life continuing. We walked to a nearby café and went online to see what the airline could do. The concert had been cancelled and our friends were no longer joining us. All I could think about was getting home, kissing my babies in their cots and seeing my parents. It was as if everything else had paled into insignificance and I knew what was really important.

We managed to get home later that day. The queues began outside the airport and snaked all the way through it. Security was strict and there was still fear in the air. I didn't relax until the plane was in the sky, only then could I really believe we were going home. My parents came to collect us at the airport – both of them, which was a testament to the seriousness of the matter – and then home to my babies. Safe, healthy, home.

I forget about this all the time. I get stressed, fed up, complacent, and I forget how the simple things in life like being at home and being safe are really all we can wish for. Normal life, the one we often say is boring, is actually beautiful.

We say 'your health is your wealth', but do we ever truly value what this means? To wake up in the morning, to put your feet on the ground if you are able, to take a breath. These are the simple things we miss when we cannot do them. It can take our health being compromised before we realise there was a before and now there is an after. No one is promised tomorrow, so every day really is a gift, even though it can be challenging to remember that sometimes.

To truly live your best life is to be in it – eyes open, heart open, feeling it all, the good, the bad and the ugly. The wellness world sells us a picture of perfection, but that doesn't exist. Life is meant to be messy, chaotic and complicated. There are ups and there are downs, navigating each one and chalking it up to experience is all any of us can do.

In 1964, Viktor Frankl in his illuminating book *Man's Search for Meaning* said that the only thing we ever really have control over is our own reaction to the things that happen around us. The book is Frankl's account of the Holocaust in which he lost his family and experienced untold horrors but remained determined to hold on to his spirit. He was a doctor of psychiatry, and his life was often spared to serve in the medical tent, where he watched those who had pinned their hopes on a day of freedom weaken and die when they gave up that hope. He made the connection between spiritual, mental and physical health. The connection between mind, body and soul.

Hope and love are two of the strongest emotions for us to hold at our core. They help to foster empathy, an understanding or appreciation for the experiences of others, however different they may be from our own.

Your best life is as unique as you, it is not for me to tell you how it should look. However, a focus on the simple things in life is as good a place as any to start.

WELL? OVER TO YOU ...

What do you love about your life? List everything from the small to the big: where you live, your family, your work, your friends, a takeaway coffee, takeaway on a Friday, a disco ball – whatever comes to mind, jot it down.

What don't you like about your life?

If you could wave a magic wand, how would your life look?

Thinking back over today – or yesterday if it's too early today – were there moments that made you smile or feel joy?

If so, what were they?

In what ways could you bring more joy into your day, your week, your life?

Pick one thing you are going to do just for yourself to bring yourself joy this week.

What one thing from the list of things you don't like in your life at the moment are you going to focus on to bring about change?

How will you go about this?

Set yourself a target for tomorrow to search for moments that make you smile or feel joy and then come back and record them here. Psychologist Allison Keating calls them 'glimmers' and I love that term. If you enjoy this process, perhaps you could start your own journal or add them to notes on your phone.

DO YOU BELIEVE IN MAGIC?

Now that we've looked at the importance of the simple things in life, can we add a sprinkle of what I like to call the magic – and being open to seeing it in our everyday?

Love, for example. Yes, there is a physical and chemical reaction taking place within us when we fall in love or feel love for another, but there's also a bit of magic that is difficult to measure. We can't accurately quantify the difference between love for a romantic partner, love for a friend and love for a child, but we know there are different types that change and evolve over time.

You have to have your radar primed for magic, keep your eyes peeled and your heart open. In Ireland, we are great at being open-hearted – there'll be a bit of craic had in the queue for the checkout, a bit of banter as you pass on the street. We love to meet a new person so we can trace them back to someone we know. Six degrees of separation has nothing on us. It is often in these fleeting conversations that connections are made, a thread that leads to something or nothing, but that shared moment can hold such power.

Do you believe in coincidence or serendipity? I like to walk around with my eyes open for opportunity. Not just for personal gain but open to the possibility of connection, of friendship, of fun and a sprinkling of luck.

When I was in my early twenties, I had begun to feel a little unfulfilled at my office job and was on the lookout for something new. I met a guy called Jonathan McCrea. I shared an apartment with Leigh, who worked in fashion, as did Jonny's then girlfriend, and, at one of their sample sales, we got chatting. It turned out he had recently made a leap from a job in IT to presenting children's television, so he became a person of great interest to me. The next time we met, I asked him even more questions and told him of my plans to make the leap too; I had started my postgrad in journalism at the time. I had been fully open to sharing exactly where I was at in life and asking him where he was at – it went beyond pleasantries as it were, to the deeper stuff. I love to go deep!

A few months later, I had left my marketing job, was working nights in a restaurant and interning at a Dublin radio station. I had been recording vox pops for the news team, heading out with a microphone to ask people their opinion on the day's topics. This is not for the faint-hearted – you get a lot of knockbacks but also you meet some great people and it's exciting to hear it on air as part of the news bulletin. I was heading home from the radio station one day and I ran into Jonny. I told him what I had been doing and he told me he was considering a move to radio. He asked if I'd be interested in recording a demo to send into stations, so of course I said 'yes'.

What we recorded led to us getting a meeting with Dublin station Spin1038, where we ended up working for seven years; the first two were at the weekends and then we got a prime-time slot presenting the lunchtime talk show. It was honestly one of the happiest times of my life: the best fun, the best partnership and my dream job. Jonny is still one of my best friends, he is godfather to my daughter and I credit him with so much of my career success. He was the driving force behind turning that demo into a meeting.

He is deeply rooted in the science world; in fact he left the talk show to pursue this part of his career and is still presenting Newstalk's science show *Futureproof*. I think it was a little bit of magic that made all that come together. How was I walking down that road at precisely the same time he was? And both of us looking for a career in radio. He'll say coincidence, I say magic.

While there is an explanation behind every magician's trick, it doesn't change the way those moments of surprise make you feel. When your card is revealed, when you get the job, when you meet the person, when your name is called out, when your wish comes true – these are the magic moments, but you have to make sure you are looking out for them.

Another more recent magic connection was when I held an event on gut-health in Dublin city centre. I really put myself out there on the night, it was the biggest event I'd hosted at the time. After we had finished, a woman came up to say hello and told me she had studied at the same college where I had received my health-coach qualification. We followed each other on Instagram and would send the odd DM; a connection was made.

The following year, I was hosting another event and Jacqueline was in the audience again. After one of the speakers had finished, she came up to say how inspired she felt and that she really wanted to bring the world-renowned speaker, author and trauma expert Dr Gabor Maté to Ireland.

She went on to win Mark Fennel's book in the raffle, it's called *Break Through*, and as I handed it to her from the stage, I whispered, 'It's your sign to make that show happen.' Now, I know I said I believe in magic, but even I didn't think that she would turn it around in a matter of months or that I would be standing on that stage as MC for Dr Gabor Maté in the RDS. But it just goes to show, you never know where each conversation might lead.

It's not all about personal or professional gain. The smile on your face from something funny someone said as they gave you your change in the shop, to the heart-warming glow that a conversation with someone can bring – be open to the magic moments in life because you never know what that spark might ignite.

LIFE-COACH CYNIC

Sometimes you can fall out of love with life, and the magic can be missing or at least difficult to see.

I've spoken earlier about the personal-development courses I went on in one of my first jobs and how they changed my view on life. Sitting in these conference halls and boardrooms learning the concept of goal-setting and visualisation was fascinating to me. Professional athletes will often use visualisation techniques to picture themselves competing, scoring the goal or the try, and winning the match. Then, when they find themselves at the defining moment, their brain has seen it before many times and so they can reduce the chance of utter panic and, in many cases, can make it happen for real.

When I sat my driving test at the age of twenty, it was just twelve weeks after my first lesson and it was intense – as I've mentioned previously, I was shocked at the challenge of taking to the roads. I'd persevered through the lessons, I had a great instructor and finally the day of the test came. I said hello to the examiner – I can still see him now – and then I excused myself to go to the bathroom before we set off. While in there, I took a moment, took a couple of deep breaths and I pictured him shaking my hand and congratulating me that I had passed. I had told no one I was taking the test that day, neither my family nor my boyfriend, who I lived with at the time, I kept my cards close to my chest. We headed off and it was all fairly textbook until a car pulled out in front of me on a hill at traffic lights. I managed to stay calm, put the handbrake on and then there was a handbrake start and off we went again – that's how I remember it anyway, but however it happened, it was an unexpected challenge and I had handled it.

We got back to the office, where he shook my hand and told me I had passed. Did that moment in the bathroom make a difference? It was added on to my lessons and efforts but I do think it helped me to remain calm and it added a sprinkle of magic to the whole experience.

As I headed out of the corporate world and into the world of radio and television, I brought this 'if you can believe it, you can achieve it' mentality with me. The knock-backs were many; sometimes, I would get calls advising me to keep going, other times I got nothing. You get jobs, lose jobs, and my trajectory was not as clear as it might have been had I stayed in marketing, but as I used to say in my catch-all line when I worked in a call centre for an internet company, 'It's the nature of the beast.'

Now, this is by no means a sob story. I have had a brilliant career with lots of fantastic opportunities and experiences. I am very happy with the life I have built for myself but I didn't always feel this way. I had been so consumed by the setting of my goals that I hadn't in any way prepared myself for when things didn't work out as I had meticulously planned them.

When you put a destination into your sat nav, you sit back and relax, assuming you'll be brought to where you want to go in the most efficient manner. So, it's frustrating to find yourself lost, driving and driving but not getting where you wanted to go. That's where I found myself; I couldn't see the wood for the trees. I remember saying to my husband one evening that perhaps things weren't working out because I needed to be more clear on my vision board, that instead of saying 'TV presenter', I should say what type of programme I wanted to present. He looked at me incredulously, as I was working on *Ireland AM* at the time. He said, 'Clare, you *are* a TV presenter.' It took me a moment to allow that to sink in. I had spent so long looking longingly at the horizon, I'd forgotten to look at where I was and how far I had come.

That's the issue that can arise with all the talk of manifesting and living your best life – we can tie ourselves up in knots trying to make it all happen and forget to actually live it. If I could go back and tweak anything, it would be my own foundation. Instead of limping off to lick my wounds when things didn't go my way, I wish I'd just bounded on to the next thing. I did get up and I did get on with it, but sometimes I limped, felt a bit sorry for myself and got a bit annoyed with the world.

That's where I was when a guest on my Newstalk show suggested I connect with her life-coach friend Aidan. She thought he would be a good feature on the show – which he was – and he offered me a free session to say thank you.

In the juggle of life, he gave me a call to get a few pointers ahead of that session while I walked up to collect my kids from school. I can still remember the way I stomped up that road, giving him what-for on the way things had not gone as I'd expected them to. I had grown totally disillusioned with the entire goal-setting process. I was doing everything right – setting the goals, doing the work – so where was my return?

I demanded that he defend the process of life coaching and how it could possibly help me. To be fair, we were in the midst of a house move in the pandemic and there was a lot going on. My dad had died after living with dementia for many years, my sister had moved to America with her husband and their two babies (my beloved niece and nephew, and my sis is my major support system) and my brother had moved to France. No wonder my sat nav was off, but the underlying thread through it all was that I felt things hadn't gone to plan. I was struggling to accept that certain work gigs that had gone during the pandemic weren't coming back. The trajectory I'd been on had changed course and my foundations had been shaken.

When we had the life-coach session, one of the exercises he asked me to do was to write my dream day five years from now, from the moment I woke up to the moment I went to sleep and everything in between. Where I woke up, who was I with? What did I do first? What did I do all day long? He told me to forget logic, just write my dream day. When I wrote it out, it was the simple things that jumped out at me – my home, my husband, my kids, those connections. Yes, there was some work stuff but there was also time – time to go for a cliff walk and a sea dip, to just be in my house.

As it was five years on, my kids were older, and when I was typing that they would be heading off to do their own thing it made my chest tighten and my stomach churn to think they wouldn't need me as much. It gave me real impetus to be in the here and now, to see the success that it is. It was such an eye-opener. And would you believe, I've started to move towards most things I wrote down that day, including this book!

I'll always be ambitious. I think we only get one, wild and precious life but that very sentiment makes me want to be fully present in the life I have now, not the life I want. They are one and the same. I think that because my thirties went by in such a flash, I decided to slow myself down in my forties, and I hope to continue that trend. Slowing down is not giving up, it's taking a moment to see what is here.

Do I sit like a Buddha with life all figured out? Absolutely not, life is constantly evolving and changing; the minute I get one part semi-sorted, another issue pops up, like whack-a-mole. But I do understand myself, I do know what is important to me and this has enabled me to be more content with where I'm at. To stop constantly checking the sat nav, asking, 'Are we there yet?' like a child from the back seat.

Instead, I'm mostly enjoying the journey. From time to time, a bottleneck of traffic can spike my stress levels and there might even be some road rage – but I catch myself, roll down the window, turn up the music and take my time. Sometimes, I get lost, sometimes I pull in and take a break, but I know I'm always on my way.

Contemplate where you are in your life. Are you striving or are you living? Is your focus so much on the horizon that you're missing the here and now? Are you so caught up in achieving and doing that you've begun to lose sight of who you truly are and what you really want? Are you stuck in a loop of blaming the world for what hasn't gone right for you so you've forgotten that you can take the reins? You can find your way back to truly being in your life and content that you know who you are. We can always set goals but it's a better starting point to be truly satisfied with where you are. Fall back in love with your life.

WELL? OVER TO YOU ...

Try the five-years-from-now exercise. On a separate piece of paper or journal write out a day in your dream life five years from now. No need for logic here, go big. How and where do you wake up? Who are you with? What's the first thing you do? Go into all the details, really see and feel it – go all the way through your day until lights out, whenever your day ends. It will give you focus, clarity and so much insight, not just about the future but about the present.

Thinking about your present-day life, consider these questions and write down what comes up for you:

Who are you?

What are the roles you play in life – from family to friends to your career if applicable?

When you take all of those away, who are you at your essence?

What three words would people use to describe you?

What three words would you use to describe yourself?

Would you describe yourself as comfortable in your own skin?

Do you have goals and plans in life you haven't made happen yet?

Why is this?

What could you do to make them happen?

What do you appreciate about what you have in life right now?

What have challenges in life taught you about yourself?

When you look at the five-years-from-now day in your life, what surprised you?

If you could pick one thing to come true from that day, what would it be?

CONNECTION

Connection is one of the foundations of our wellbeing and I've placed it here in the Soul section as the people in our life can truly light us up. A sense of belonging, of community, is the lifeblood of what it means to be human.

From our family of origin to the family we choose for ourselves with our friends to the community of the wider world, when we connect with these people and feel a part of something it creates meaning and purpose in our lives.

Technology has us more connected than ever before and yet loneliness and isolation is an epidemic in the modern age. The answer is not to throw your tech away because, while there are times I wish we all could, it's not realistic. The antidote is to make sure we lean in to real-life human connection. The world may have evolved around us but, at our core, we are tribal people who need to feel like we belong. The power of connecting over a shared experience, coming together with like-minded people over a conversation, on a dancefloor, in a muddy field at a festival is the essence of what it means to be human, to connect.

The feeling when people come together to celebrate love at a wedding or to celebrate life and commiserate at a funeral is one we all need. The pandemic taught us so much about the power of a hug, a chat in a bank queue or even being able to see someone's entire face, mask-free – it's the social fabric of who we are.

In the tribes of old, all generations would come together; the saying 'it takes a village' was literally born out of that sense of community, working and raising families together. Today, we don't make as much time for our neighbours, we are so busy scrolling, looking at people we don't really know.

I've had the privilege of interviewing Capuchin Franciscan priest-friar Brother Richard Hendrick in recent years on the publication of his two brilliant books *Still Points* and *Calming the Storms*. What I love about Brother Richard is that while he does live quite a different life to many of us in that much of his day is mapped out with time for meditation and prayer, he is not that far removed from everyday life because of his work within the community – and he also has a smartphone that he says occasionally pulls him in too.

He once told me of a time when he was upstairs on a double-decker bus looking out the window, surrounded by people. At a set of lights, there was a man with a leaf blower he was struggling to control but was having a bit of fun with it. This jovial scene caused Brother Richard to smile and he turned to his fellow travellers on the bus to see if there was someone else to share a smile with and everyone had their heads down, looking at their phones.

Now, this leaf-blower scene is by no means a life-or-death situation, but how many smiles are we missing?

A clip came up on my phone recently – yes, I was scrolling – of a woman being interviewed by Oprah about her book. In it, she had documented a time when her young daughters had called her into their bedroom one night and said, 'Mom, where are you? You are here but you are not here.' Turns out, it was a massive awakening for this woman that eventually unearthed a past trauma in her life, but that question actually stopped me in my tracks. 'Mom, where are you? You are here but you are not here.' How many of us are here but not here for the people that we truly love?

The times when I have been short with my kids have often been the ones when I'm most stretched. That can't always be helped – we are all doing the best we can – but there were times when I was answering an email, trying to cook dinner and the constant calling of 'Mom' tipped me over the edge. Why wasn't it the email that tipped me over the edge? Put down the phone, do what thousands of people the world over did for thousands of years – when they came in the door they left work behind and were home.

In bed at night are you scrolling on your phone rather than chatting with your partner? Those little chats are part of the necessary intimacy that fuels long-term relationships.

Are you making time for your friends? Proper time for a phone call, a coffee, a walk? Are you putting yourself out there to meet new people who light you up?

We have a finite amount of energy, it is true, and many of us have social batteries that run down more quickly than others, but if we feel we don't have time for the people in our lives, then we need to look at how we are spending our time. Often, we are tired because we are lacking joy, not just because we are busy.

The best way is to start small. Commit to one friend or one family meet-up a month if that is all you can manage. A quick cup of tea, it doesn't have to cost the earth. Get outside with a group of your pals if you can, walk the beach, have a coffee or suggest a game of something you love but have let slip.

Be mindful of the people you spend your time with. Not everyone in your life can light you up and often that has more to do with what is going on for them than you, but make sure that for every draining energy you encounter, you try to balance it out with someone who makes you laugh, someone who gives great advice, a great hug or someone who just gets you.

We may need to schedule this time in the same way we

schedule a dentist appointment or a work meeting, treating the moments of connection with the same respect and priority. We might scoff at the concept of date night but it's important to water our flowers if we want them to bloom – and, no, that's not a euphemism!

If my husband and I have been like ships passing each other, only we're more like pirate ships, shouting from one bow to the other about which kid needed to be dropped where, then it's time for us to either go out as a couple or head out with our friends. Have a laugh, hold hands and be reminded that there was a spark that led to those kids in the first place.

I'm conscious you might be reading this as a single parent or perhaps there are major financial worries on your plate every single day. You are pushed to your maximum with whatever this chapter in your life is serving you. I get that it's not always easy to throw your coat on and head out the door for 'me time'. But these are the times we need connection most. However small, reaching out to connect to a support group online or in person is the first step to easing that burden as you realise you are not alone. None of us are, this planet is jam-packed.

And if it is just normal modern life that has you run ragged like the rest of us, then slow down, take a moment. Take in the people who are around you. Suggest a meet-up IRL ASAP. It's good for the soul and your wellbeing.

WELL? OVER TO YOU ...

Make a list of all the important people in your life.

Who from this list lights you up?

Why?

Who on the list can be draining?

Why?

Do you prioritise spending time with those on the light-up list?

How could you better manage those who don't? (This might be a conversation, a boundary or just an awareness of how much time you give to these people and thinking about them.)

Would you consider yourself as someone who values and takes care of your friendships?

Are there ways you could do better here?

If so, what are they?

If you feel you are lacking in friends you can trust and have fun with – what could you do to meet more like-minded people?

A great way to mind your relationships is to figure out what you look for in one. We all have different love languages based on our life experiences and they may differ from those of our friends and romantic partner. Rather than feel let down if our language isn't the same, we can try to understand and appreciate where the other person is coming from and why it's impacting on us the way it is.

For example, you might be someone who really likes to show affection physically through hugging or hand-holding but your partner or friend might not feel the same. Their not wanting to hug you isn't an indication that they're not that into you, it's just who they are.

> Check out your love language on 5lovelanguages.com.

JOY

We need joy in our lives, something that is often missing from the health-and-wellness message. Even though it is an essential part of what makes us tick as humans, we have been sold the story that it has to be difficult to be effective – remember, 'No pain, no gain'? While I am all for personal challenge and pushing yourself outside of your comfort zone, there needs to be an element of enjoyment, otherwise why on earth would we want to do it? So much of our wellbeing is centred around small things that, done consistently, over time build to make a big difference. So, if it brings you joy, you are far more likely to stick with it.

How often have you said on a Sunday that next week is going to be different? You might clear out your treat cupboard, the contents may even get eaten for one last hurrah before the first day of the rest of your life. You pledge to never allow sugar into the house again and snacking is now a thing of the past. Monday you are a blaze of motivation with a low-calorie breakfast, maybe even just a green juice, you get out for a walk or a run before work and, for lunch, you'll just have soup. That evening, the wok is dusted down for the reliable stir fry and you head off to bed feeling victorious. Is it any wonder that by Wednesday you feel like giving up and perhaps by the weekend you have, because living that way is not fun and is not sustainable.

Health and wellness are not supposed to be a stick for us to beat ourselves with or something else that we are failing at. If we truly look to better our wellbeing, it's about nourishing ourselves, mind, body and soul, investing in our future so we can feel as good as we can for as long as we can. That means eating nutrient-rich foods and lots of them, the foods we mentioned when looking at gut health – plenty of fibre, fruit, veg, pulses, lean meats, wholegrains, fermented foods, and eating the rainbow of balanced meals containing protein, carbohydrate and fat. It means moving our bodies in a way that we enjoy and it means that we minimise our stress levels; joy is the fuel injector your efforts need.

Along with all of this, we need to think about what feeds our soul. What speaks to the essence of who we are and what lights us up.

Sometimes, we can feel worn out because we have been doing too much, but often we can feel exhausted because we haven't been doing what lights us up and we haven't been having enough fun. Just because we grow older doesn't mean we have to throw away all playfulness. It's important to be silly and feel free. This can come from having belly laughs with friends, connecting on a pitch or on a dancefloor, engaging in a pastime you adored but haven't made time for. Where does joy feature in your life and where is it missing?

Often you won't notice the joy has slipped away, so how do you know it's gone? For me, it has come with that constant check-in. When I notice myself feeling overwhelmed and weary, I'm snapping at the kids and short with my husband. I don't have the energy for the things I usually enjoy and there's a sense of dragging myself through the week. I take it as a message, an opportunity to slow down and look at how I've been living. Have I been running on empty, letting good food and quality sleep slip? Have I been working too much, saying 'yes' to too many things not realising that it means I'm saying 'no' to something else? Where has joy been in my week or my month?

We all have times in our lives when things ramp up, when it's harder to even consider fun and we scramble to get through a stressful situation. But these are the times we need to lean in even more. Recently, I had a group for a six-week online course and each of the ten people had major life stuff going on. From relationship breakdown to feeling stuck in a career to facing retirement and unsure of what this chapter would bring. There was one gorgeous person who was her mother's live-in carer; at the weekends her supportive siblings would help too but, instead of taking time for herself, she would spend the weekend at work in a busy retail store. Her days were spent thinking of her mother's needs, from medication to meals to spending time with her, something we could all see was very important and valued. While there were times she would head out to the cinema or the theatre, I had been asking the group to consider ways in which they could incorporate time just for themselves, ten minutes a day and if joy could be in there, even better.

It was autumn when I held the course and, one evening, this beautiful carer said she had been making time to head for a walk, even a short one, to make sure she took time for herself. She told us how one day she had kicked the crunchy fallen leaves and asked rather hesitantly if that was joy. I asked how it had made her feel. She said it reminded her of being a child, it was fun, she felt free and maybe a bit silly. For that moment, she wasn't thinking of the responsibility on her shoulders or how she would continue to manage, she was just kicking leaves and smiling – that's joy for sure. It doesn't have to be a massive undertaking, a trip or a big night out, joyful though they are, it can be moments as simple as kicking fallen leaves on a bright autumn day.

WELL? OVER TO YOU ...

What in life brings you joy?

How often does joy feature in your week?

If you feel it is lacking, what gets in the way?

When was the last time you said, 'That was good for my soul'?

What were you doing?

How could you bring more fun or joy into your life?

LET'S HAVE A RECAP

So, what are the messages I hope you take with you from reading this book? Overall, I hope you've begun to have a mindset shift about what health and wellness is, empowered to make small changes that are unique to you so that you can feel as good as you can for as long as you can.

I hope you now better understand that, although the advice is simple, it is not always simple to execute, as life is complicated and we are complex.

The best advice I can give you is to go gently. The smallest of steps will help you to break things down, remain motivated and build over time to make a big difference. Be kind to yourself; nourishing yourself means taking care of yourself, not pushing too hard, but also making sure you are giving yourself what you truly need – mind, body and soul. Often, we think to go gentle on ourselves means we lose the run of ourselves altogether and that we will remain on the couch day after day ordering takeaways, but while that is a nice thing to do from time to time, doing it all the time will become tedious and begin to chip away at our sense of wellbeing.

If we find ourselves continually choosing behaviours and habits that aren't making us feel good and we are struggling to make a change, then it can be worth getting support to figure out what's at the centre of your decision-making. Support from a friend or professional, whether it's meeting for more regular walks or a class or just as a listening ear and accountability partner.

One January, I had the fabulous navigation coach Tara Rafter on the show to try and dissuade people from New Year's resolutions that would be hard to stick to. She said that peace is the new success. To put your head on the pillow at night content with the day you have had and to wake up the following morning looking forward to what's to come is the most we can hope for in life. We don't have to go around like a character from a storybook, all singing and all dancing, calling in the woodland creatures as we go, but a general self-knowing that you are doing your best and being open to growth is a foundation that will serve you well as you navigate the ups and downs of life.

Bryan Johnson is a tech billionaire, who, upon selling his business, turned his attention to the world of longevity and biohacking. He is the subject of a Netflix documentary and is now constantly surrounded by machines and a team of scientists researching how to delay and, at times, reverse his biological age and to see how far they can extend a healthy lifespan.

Every calorie he consumes is rigorously studied and chosen, he stops eating at 11 a.m. every day to optimise his sleep and he does not allow himself sunlight at all. I saw him first on an episode of *The Kardashians*. They were gathered around a table for a meal of lentils, grains and broccoli and he asked his guests to consider what they'd do if they were handed the prescription for what would guarantee them the longest life possible. The prescription would be detailed and disciplined and would have to be followed to the letter. They all chorused that yes they would do it, and the scientists also seated at the table were salivating at the prospect but, for me, it's a hard no. While I am interested in what can help me to live a long and healthy life, I don't want that to come with a rigid plan, I don't think that is living. I get that Bryan Johnson is putting himself forward as a scientific guinea pig and, perhaps, ran out of ideas for what to do with his money but, from what I could see, his life lacked fun, flexibility, spontaneity and, if I'm honest, joy.

Diagnostic technologies are set to grow, with more scanning and testing to get ahead of the game, and while screening saves lives, a constant obsession with how healthy we are is, I feel, leaning towards the unhealthy.

The danger of living this way and often the message of the wellness world is that we are sold the possibility of a perfect life – one where everything is in balance, we are thriving physically, mentally and emotionally. But real life doesn't work that way; it is messy and chaotic and constantly changing, like the weather. All we can do is our best to make sure we are equipped to take on whatever comes our way, but sometimes we are going to get caught in the rain. This doesn't mean you are doing life wrong; in fact, it means you are living it.

The pursuit of perfection will always leave you lacking because perfection simply doesn't exist. People can do incredible things and achieve so much, but getting sick, feeling tired and having down days are all part of life.

I once interviewed a psychotherapist who worked mainly with people at varying stages of their cancer journey. He said so many sat in front of him and asked why they had their diagnosis and if it could be because they didn't know how to process their emotions properly. Those words made me feel so sad and have stayed with me. There should be no guilt and shame in any diagnosis. Yes, sometimes an illness can be a catalyst for looking at and living life a bit differently but it doesn't mean it was your fault.

Let me remind you that we are all doing the best we can with what we've got. So, where do you go from here?

Start by giving yourself the space to truly listen to yourself.

Tune in to what you need and tune out all the noise and the negative self-talk.

Let's try it now ...

Read through the exercise first and then get ready to check in with yourself.

- Start by bring awareness to your breath as it is now.
- Feel your sit bones on the chair, your feet on the ground or your body against the couch and take three deep breaths with a focus on a long, slow exhale.
- Now ask yourself – how do I feel? Close your eyes or lower you gaze and listen to what comes up.
- What one word would you use to describe how you feel right now?
- Are you surprised by this answer?
- What do you think has led to this being your choice of word and this feeling?
- What are your feelings about this – are you meeting this with any emotions?
- How do you speak to yourself in your mind day to day?
- Is your inner voice kind?
- Would you say you back yourself and show up for yourself?
- Do you treat yourself as a best friend?
- If not, why not?
- Again take three deep breaths with a focus on the long, slow exhale.

Try to weave this exercise into your day at least once. The more conscious you become of how you are feeling and how you are speaking to yourself, the more able you will be to notice your inner dialogue and how helpful it is to you.

Remember that your wellness blueprint is unique to you, so take the time to figure out what works for you and what doesn't. Like the breakfast buffet in a fancy hotel, we can get overwhelmed by all the delights on offer but remember what it feels like when your plate is overloaded. When you've flipped from the breakfast basics of eggs and bacon and now they sit alongside pastries, desserts and maybe even sushi! (Just me?!) You sit down at the table unsure of where to start, wishing you hadn't worried about what people would think and just went up loads of times, each time with a smaller plate, trying one course at a time. Piling everything on the plate all at once is overwhelming. I'm all for giving everything a go, including sushi for breakfast, but a slower pace means you can take on every experience and make an informed choice.

There is a sweet spot between being on it when it comes to your wellbeing and being obsessed. This comes from having self-awareness and a strong foundation that enables you to be flexible as life happens around you.

Holiday you

This is an important one in the recap as it's one last mindset shift that might just soften your life focus. What are some of the ways in which you behave on holiday that you could bring into your every day?

It's rather fitting that I am writing this chapter on a flight home from a week in sunny Spain. It was a well-needed holiday with my family, a chance to unwind, relax, recharge and have some time together.

There have been times on various holidays over the years where I have caught my reflection in the mirror and thought, *There she is, there is the real me, relaxed and calm.* I often pack multiple outfits, my make-up, the hair curler and most of the time it all gets left in the wardrobe in favour of simple clothes, wet hair and a slick of lip balm. Happy to just be.

Obviously, there are things that make this relaxed, calm me happen: the lack of work, the change of scenery, the weather. Of course, you're going to be chilled when the main stress you have for the day is deciding between the pool or the beach. Heading out in the evenings for dinner, uninvolved in its preparation, a glass of wine or a small beer with lunch perhaps and sleeping in with no alarm.

These are things you can't bring into your everyday, I grant you, but have you ever considered ways in which you could bring 'holiday you' home? On holiday, you spend a lot of time outside – whether that's sightseeing or sitting on your balcony in the morning sun. Can you do that more at home? Get outside, take a walk in the morning or sit in the garden with your cup of tea. On the less palatable days, can you watch the storm from your window or wrap up to face the elements? As they say, there's no such thing as bad weather, just bad clothing.

On holiday, you allow for long periods of rest, sunning yourself, reading a book or doing a crossword. Can you do that at home? You might not have the sun in the sky but can you allow yourself to rest, to read for longer than the two to three pages before you conk out at the end of your day?

On holiday, we give ourselves permission to rest, to relax the rules and have fun. Can you bring that into your everyday a little more? I'm not suggesting your significant other comes home to a jug of sangria and a giant paella pot of a Tuesday necessarily, although that does sound like fun – it's more a state of mind that you bring into how you live every day rather than just saving it for the week or two a year. You deserve more than that.

So, when we land in an hour or so and head home, I won't lament the end of the holiday, although I will miss those balmy temperatures. I will be happy to have made the memories and will keep the sparkle of holiday Clare for as long as I can. You can bring a sense of holiday into home life too.

What to keep an eye on

As you move forward, hopefully with a changed or sharpened mindset when it comes to your health and wellbeing, what can you use to monitor how well you are?

Toilet habits

Even though there is still a bit of a taboo around this, and granted it isn't really a dinner-party-friendly discussion, everybody 'spends a penny' or more and it can be a fairly good indication of how your digestive health is, which will impact how you feel.

Let's start with your pee. We've become obsessed with staying hydrated with a selection of water containers on the market to rival Imelda Marcos and her infamous shoe collection but, essentially – and this is coming from a serious water drinker herself – the best way to know if you are drinking enough is to check out the colour of your pee. Straw-coloured yellow, with a decent flow, and you're good. Anything darker in colour and a mere trickle and you may need more water. Eight glasses a day is recommended but everyone is different; you can also get your water intake from other sources including tea and even coffee, although that is considered a diuretic, which means it makes you pee.

If you struggle to drink water, then add fruit to it to change up the flavour. It can also be easier to drink when it is at room temperature rather than ice cold, and herbal tea can be a great way to up your intake.

Type 1	Hard lumps or small pebbles
Type 2	Lumpy, hard and sausage shaped
Type 3	Sausage shaped with cracks along the surface
Type 4	Resembles a thin sausage or snake
Type 5	Soft blobs with clear edges
Type 6	Mushy and fluffy with ragged edges
Type 7	Entirely liquid

Figure 6: The Bristol stool chart

When it comes to what is known as your number two (who knows why), the Bristol Stool Chart goes into great detail on what the consistency of what is in the bowl can tell us about our digestive system.

If you are Type 1 or 2, chances are you are constipated, while 5, 6 or 7 indicate stools that are too loose. This can happen to everybody from time to time, but if this is happening the majority of the time it's worth making an appointment to see your GP. Your stools are a great indication of how things are with your gut health and overall health. Everybody is different. It is important that you know what your normal is, so that if you feel anything has changed you can look at what has been going on in life – what you've been eating, how you've been eating, what you've been drinking, your stress levels, hormone fluctuation. All of these, and more, can play a role and may give you some direction on changes to make, but ultimately any changes if persistent should be checked out by your GP.

There is nothing to be embarrassed about here, GPs have seen and heard it all and they go to the loo regularly too.

Your energy levels

How are you feeling from day to day? Are you waking up refreshed or are you still exhausted even after what you would consider to be a good night's sleep? Can you get through the demands of your life with a reasonable amount of energy or do you find that you're dragging yourself along?

There may be lots of reasonable explanations as to why we can have dips in our energy, from young children to work deadlines to shift work to stressful seasons in our life. These times will come and go but if your energy levels are consistently at a low ebb then it is worth considering what is contributing to this and if there are tweaks you can make. How are you eating? Are you eating enough and giving your body the fuel it needs? Are you moving your body? Often when we feel exhausted, it is sleep and rest that we need but, conversely, often moving more and doing more exercise will energise us rather than deplete us.

It's the self-awareness and your inner dialogue that will help you to judge which of these you need.

I suggest that if you are introducing movement to energise yourself, you start slowly, no need to go from couch to 5 km in one day. You will know what movement appeals to you and is right for you, but I would suggest a walk in nature: your local park, beach or forest – keep it short and see how you feel after it.

Being tired all the time is one of the most common reasons people go to their GP – I know because my own GP told me this when I sat in front of her with that very complaint. I wanted, as we all often do, to be prescribed a magic pill that would instantly energise me, enabling me to take on the world with ease, but there isn't one. Instead, it's a return to the basics of nutrition, movement, sleep and stress management and, in some cases, further investigation in the form of a blood test to rule out any other causes. Again, knowing your normal, being aware when something has changed and doesn't feel right and seeking support and medical advice is so important.

Remember, not feeling like yourself is enough of a symptom for a GP visit.

Your fun diary

Sometimes, we can feel tired because we are doing too much and need to slow down, to take time to rest and recharge. But at other times we can feel exhausted because we haven't been making enough time for any joy or fun. We can't keep toiling on the treadmill of life without occasionally stepping off to just be silly and to do the things that light us up.

Here is another instance when it isn't black and white, and you will have to rely on your own intuition to inform your decision. There have been so many times before a night out or even a weekend away where I will say to myself, 'I could do without this.' I'm already so overwhelmed with everything I've got going on that to pack for a trip to any destination and to summon the energy to show up and have fun seems like too much. Then, I get there and almost every time when I'm out of the house and having fun, I wonder what on earth I was thinking. When you're feeling like having fun will tip you over the overwhelmed edge, chances are you need it more than ever.

Finding what fun means to you goes far beyond pints in the pub or a nightclub dancefloor. It's a sense of letting go, of doing what lights you up, often with people you love. It's important and needs to be scheduled in like any dental appointment or work meeting.

How much time you spend on your phone

I'm as guilty as anyone else of spending time on my phone. We live in the modern world, don't we, where most of our lives are contained in those rectangular devices we carry around with us. Even when we go on holiday, I think that I'll leave my phone in a drawer and take a break from it, but all the bookings are on it and I use it to pay for everything – we are hooked.

If you're not, I salute you – it's not easy to be conscious of how much we are sucked into scrolling the never-ending stream of information coming at us. Technology has helped us in so many ways, but it has begun to encroach upon the way we are designed to live. It's keeping us in, keeping us isolated and distracting us from our own needs.

Social media can be such a fun and inspiring place, but it can also leave you feeling like you're not enough in a way we never would have before it came into our lives. Curate your feed to accounts that make you feel good and mute the ones that don't.

Keep an eye on how often you reach for your phone and be sure it's not replacing time with family, friends, being out moving or out in nature. You'll know what level is right for you.

Your relationships

Are you looking after the people in your life and are they looking after you? This can be complicated, I know, not everyone is dealt a hand of perfect family and friendships. It's clichéd but the most important relationship you have is with yourself and feeling like you are enough on your own, and that everyone else is an added bonus.

Our relationships shape us, from the family we are born into to the ones we choose for ourselves. They can light up our lives but also cause the greatest of darkness. Only you will know where you are with yours. Are there people in your life you need to see more of? Or less of? Are you surrounding yourself with positive people who make you feel good about yourself? Do you feel supported, seen and heard? Do you have people in your life to have fun with and to let go of life's stresses with? Do you have people you can trust and rely on?

If you don't have any of these people, are you minding yourself through this and seeking support? It's not a quick fix to step away from relationships that are no longer serving us but by getting your own foundation as strong as possible and leaning on supports – professional support may be the first port of call – you can find a way to better days. You deserve them.

If you have beautiful relationships, take care of them. It can be so easy to take the people in your life for granted – like plants, the more you water them, the more likely they are to bloom.

Friendships can change, it's one thing I've learned through the decades. While you may well have your diehards from your schooldays, it can be trickier to spend time with them in your forties and beyond in the way you did in your teens and twenties – life ebbs and flows and friendships are part of that. I always think the best friends are the ones you can pick up with where you left off, no matter how long it's been since you've spoken to them, and can be 100 per cent yourself. These friendships deserve care and attention – you get as much as you give.

Romantic relationships can change too, people can grow apart or situations can alter. I wish we celebrated the single life more – and what a stunning time it can be. We don't need another person to validate our worth.

Often, if we are romantically entwined, we put a huge amount of pressure on our significant other to be all things to us. I have a gorgeous husband who is amazing, but he is part of the jigsaw of my life and I of his. Everyone from my family to my friends to my work mates to my therapist, my listeners, strangers I meet along the way – they make up a tapestry of what I need in life. To expect one person to be your confidante, your organiser, your entertainment, your lover and your friend is a lot for that person to manage on their own.

So, keep an eye on your relationships, they tell you a lot about where you are at in life. And if you're not minding them and they are not minding you, what needs to change?

Your time to yourself

You need time on your own. It can seem impossible, especially if you are in the trenches of young family life, but time by yourself is essential. Time to just be still or silent and just do you.

How you spend this time will ultimately be up to you. A walk listening to a podcast, time at the gym, a swim or a date just for you. I had a pal who did that once a week for a year, she would go to the cinema, see a play or have a meal on her own, and she loved it. Why do we think people will care if you are sitting by yourself having a meal in a restaurant? I often wonder why we find it impossible to just sit with ourselves if we are at a bus stop or are first in the pub, that we feel compelled to take out our phones to check nonsense rather than just take a moment to simply be.

When I had very small kids, babies in particular, I used to love going to the supermarket on my own. Strolling around the aisles, swaying to the piped-in music and then thrilled in the silent car constantly looking in the rear-view mirror to check on a child who wasn't there. We need time by ourselves.

Make a date with yourself at least once a week to do something just for you. I'm a proponent of the daily check-in with yourself, ten minutes a day to see how you are and what you might need – just 1 per cent of your day to figure out how things are going. This time to yourself is different, it's a reset and recharge moment just for you. I'm a big fan of a potter around the house, putting things away and just doing my own thing, but I think that's just housework. Find out what works for you and invest in yourself and time on your own. You're worth it.

And, most importantly – tune in

Do you follow your intuition? Do you trust that you have an inner knowing? It's often described as a 'gut feeling' and more and more evidence is emerging about the gut–brain connection. We know how the thoughts we have impact on our physical self as well as our behaviours. If you feel nervous, you will often have an elevated heart rate and 'butterflies' in your tummy.

We are also energetic beings. We can often read the energy in the room: if you've walked in on a row – or the opposite, the frisson of excitement when two strangers lock eyes – there's an energy. There are situations where we just feel uncomfortable or times we have a feeling something isn't quite right; it stings when we ignore our gut feeling on something. We put so much weight behind what our head is saying and there is merit to the logical brain, but what is the heart saying? What of our inner voice?

I picture you reading the last page and putting the book down on the nightstand or table and thinking, *I can do this*. But it must go beyond the thinking. The plan is going to be unique to you, but it must start with an action, one step forward, showing up for yourself and doing what you say you are going to do. I promise you, as you take the small steps and build over time, it just becomes who you are and it's not something you have to give as much thought and effort to as you do at the beginning.

Don't compare and despair. Don't worry about what other people are doing or saying or where they are at in life. Stay in your own lane, go at your own pace with your own destination – you do you.

The people in your life can sometimes be thrown when you start to make changes. It unsettles them, it might cause them to look at their own life, so you might get some comments that at times may seem unsupportive. But everyone is doing the best they can where they are at. Answer their questions if you feel like it, let the comments bounce off you if you don't feel they are helpful, and stay on your own path.

Keep the mantra of nourishing yourself at the core of every action you take, because you love yourself and you deserve to feel as good as you can for as long as you can.

I wish you well.

WELL? OVER TO YOU ...

Start thinking about what your plan is – remember, it's unique to you and small steps build up over time. Removing overwhelm is the mission, keep it simple and keep it kind.

Do you feel you've had a mindset shift when it comes to health and wellness?

What has changed for you?

What ways of thinking or unhelpful habits are you going to leave behind?

What areas would you like to focus on going forward? (Tick where appropriate – as many as you like but you will eventually need to pick one or two to zone in on.)

- Movement
- Sleep
- Stress management
- Rest and restorative practice
- Connection

- Joy
- Nutrition
- Career
- Physical health
- Mental health
- Spirituality

Now, of those that you have ticked, pick which one you are going to focus on first.

What steps would you like to take to bring change here? Map them all out. For example, Mental health: *I will try/return to talk therapy.*
- Spend fifteen minutes researching therapists in your area.
- Find out if you are eligible for free support via work or medical card or are covered on medical insurance.
- Make a phone call to ask any questions.
- Make an appointment.
- See how you feel after the first appointment and, if happy, book in however many sessions you and your therapist feel is necessary.

Tick these off the list as you go, congratulate yourself and keep checking in on how you feel.

For the second area you'd like to focus in on, list the steps you will take. Continue this as you begin to bring tweaks of change to your life. And enjoy the process: remember, it's not linear and you're not competing for a prize – go gently.

Where are you going to prioritise rest in your day and week?

Where are you going to make time for joy and fun in your week and month?

How do you speak to yourself?

Does it need change?

Where will you start – e.g. affirmations, gratitude list?

EXERCISES

Take some time to work out your strengths and values using the following two exercises, then use the Circle of Life tool to build a solid foundation. They can be really helpful, not only to understand ourselves better but also to help us make decisions. I have mine written and printed on my home office wall.

Strengths exercise

First, let's start by recognising our strengths by taking a survey. The Character Strengths Survey from the University of Pennsylvania can be found here: www.authentichappiness.sas.upenn.edu/testcenter.

1. Scroll down to title box 'Engagement Questionnaires'.
2. Within this list click on the third option, 'Via Survey of Character Strengths' TAKE TEST.

3. Then you will be prompted to register your account.
4. Then take the test.
5. Results will be generated; screengrab/print.

Values exercise

1. Determine your core values. In the list on the next page, circle each core value that resonates with you. Do not overthink your selection. As you read through the list, simply write down the words that feel like a core value to you personally. If you think of a value you possess that is not on the list, add it at the end.
2. Group all similar values together from the list of values you have just created. Group them in a way that makes sense to you, personally. Create a maximum of five groups. If you have more than five groups, drop those least important to you. See the example below.

Abundance	Acceptance	Appreciation	Balance	Cheerfulness
Growth	Compassion	Encouragement	Health	Fun
Wealth	Inclusiveness	Thankfulness	Personal Development	Happiness
Security	Intuition	Thoughtfulness	Spirituality	Humour
Freedom	Kindness	Mindfulness	Wellbeing	Inspiration
Independence	Love			Joy
Flexibility	Making a Difference			Optimism
Peace				Playfulness
	Openmindedness			
	Trusworthiness			
	Relationships			

Abundance	Curiosity	Intelligence	Relationships
Accepteance	Daring	Intuition	Reliability
Accountability	Decisiveness	Joy	Resilience
Achievement	Dedication	Kindness	Resourcefulness
Advancement	Dependability	Knowledge	Responsibility
Adventure	Diversity	Leadership	Responsiveness
Advocacy	Empathy	Learning	Risk Taking
Ambition	Encouragement	Love	Safety
Appreciation	Enthusiasm	Loyalty	Security
Attractiveness	Ethics	Making a Difference	Self-Control
Autonomy	Excellence	Mindfulness	Selflessness
Balance	Expressiveness	Motivation	Service
Being the Best	Fariness	Optimism	Spirituality
Benevolence	Family	Openmindedness	Stability
Boldness	Friendships	Originality	Simplicity
Brilliance	Flexibiliy	Passion	Stability
Calmness	Freedom	Peace	Success
Challenge	Fun	Perfection	Thankfulness
Charity	Grace	Performance	Thoughtfulness
Cheerfulness	Growth	Personal Development	Traditionalism
Cleverness	Happiness	Playfulness	Trustworthiness
Community	Health	Popularity	Understanding
Commitment	Honesty	Power	Uniqueness
Compassion	Humility	Preparedness	Usefulness
Co-operation	Humour	Proactivity	Versatility
Collaboration	Incluseiveness	Professionalism	Vision
Consistency	Independence	Punctuality	Warmth
Contribution	Individuality	Quality	Wealth
Creativity	Innovation	Recognition	Wisdom
Credibility	Inspiration		Zeal

3. Choose one word within each group that best represents the label for the entire group. Again, do not overthink your labels. There are no right or wrong answers. you are defining the answer that is right for you. See the example below.

Abundance	Acceptance	Appreciation	Balance	Cheerfulness
Growth	Compassion	Encouragement	Health	Fun
Wealth	Inclusiveness	Thankfulness	Personal Development	**Happiness**
Security	Intuition	Thoughtfulness	Spirituality	Humour
Freedom	Kindness	**Mindfulness**	**Wellbeing**	Inspiration
Independence	Love			Joy
Flexibility	**Making a Difference**			Optimism
Peace				Playfulness
	Openmindedness			
	Trusworthiness			
	Relationships			

The Circle of Life tool

Now, let's help you identify and build your own solid foundation by looking at the following tool.

This is the Circle of Life tool from the Institute of Integrative Nutrition. These are the primary foods – the parts of life to consider before looking at secondary foods which is what is on your plate.

1. Imagine there is a one at the centre of each segment and a ten at the outside line, one being not good at all and ten being excellent – the line under each section correlates to that part of life.

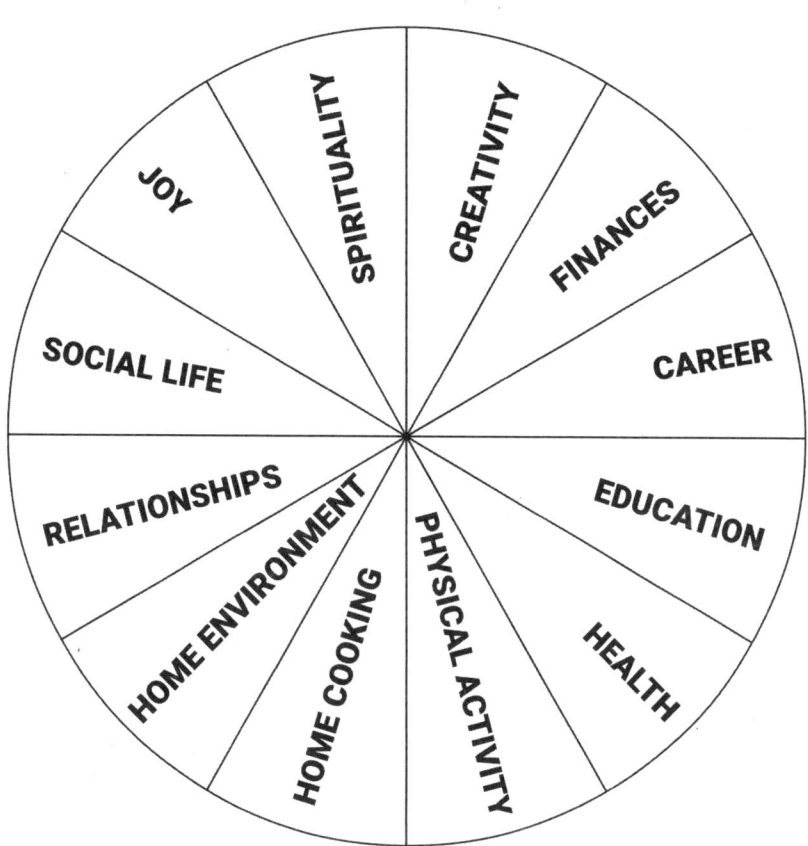

Figure 7: The Circle of Life tool

2. Ask yourself, 'How do I feel things are going in this area?' and plot where you are between one and ten. Do this without judgement, this is all brilliant knowledge to have and an essential starting point if you want to introduce any change. I promise you, there is no one on the planet who is at a ten with each section all of the time.

3. Pick your point for each one and then join up the dots; the squiggly line you end up with will give you an indication of which areas need the most attention. I recommend delving into two areas at a time. There is no point trying to overhaul everything all at once; we are trying to avoid the overwhelm, not increase it.

4. Pick the two areas you would like to work with most. Write them with the following headings:
   - Area 1
   - Area 2

   Underneath jot down anything that comes to mind that you'd like to introduce or change here.

5. Now look back at what you've jotted down – is there one thing from each list you can make into an actionable step? Start small – it might be researching something online such as a new class or joining a group, let the research be the first step. Perhaps it's making a phone call or scheduling a meeting. Do you need to have a conversation with a family member or your workplace? Map out what you'd like to say and what you would hope to achieve.

   Perhaps you would like to do more home cooking – start with one breakfast, one lunch or one dinner in a week and build slowly from there. If it's a sort out of your home environment, choose one little corner or area to begin with – it has to be small and achievable for us to make it happen.

6. Over a three-month period, keep chipping away at these two areas and allow the changes to bed in; you can reassess every month and even return to the circle of life and record any changes. Give it time and go easy on yourself. Change is challenging but can be so rewarding – it's not about success but about understanding yourself better. The main goal is to get life flow as well as it can so that you feel as good as you can.

BIBLIOGRAPHY

Abookire, Susan, 'Can forest therapy enhance health and well-being?'. 2020. www.health.harvard.edu/blog/can-forest-therapy-enhance-health-and-well-being-2020052919948.

Beresford-Kroeger, Diana, *To Speak for the Trees*. Timber Press, 2021.

Blue zones, www.bluezones.com

Buettner, Dan, *The Blue Zones*, 2nd edition. National Geographic, 2012.

Buettner, Dan, *The Blue Zones Solution*. National Geographic, 2015.

Cameron, Julia, *The Artist's Way*. Atlantic Press, 1992.

Davey, Daniel, *Eat Up: The Next Level*. Gill Books, 2022.

Day, Elizabeth, *How to Fail with Elizabeth Day* podcast. Elizabeth Day and Sony Music Entertainment.

de Mello, Anthony, *Awareness*. Bantam Doubleday Dell Publishing Group, 2000.

Doyle, Glennon, *Untamed*. Vermilion, 2020.

Fildes, Alison *et al.*, 'Probability of an Obese Person Obtaining Normal Body Weight; Cohort Study using Electronic Health Records'. *American Journal of Public Health*, 105(9), September 2015.

Frankl, Viktor, *Man's Search for Meaning*. Hodder & Stoughton, 1964.

Freudenberger, Herbert & North, Gail, 'Burn-out bei Frauen.' *Über das Gefühl des Ausgebranntseins*.12, 1992.

Ganipisetti V.M. & Bollimunta P., *Obesity and Set-Point Theory* (Updated 2023, Apr 25). In: StatPearls [Internet]. Treasure Island (FL): StatPearls Publishing; Jan 2025.

Globalwellnessinstitute.org: https://globalwellnessinstitute.org/what-is-wellness/history-of-wellness.

Hari, Johann, *Magic Pill*. Bloomsbury Publishing, 2024.

Hendrick, Brother Richard, *Still Points*. Hachette Books Ireland, 2022.

Hendrick, Brother Richard, *Calming the Storms*. Hachette Books Ireland, 2024.

Keng S.L., Smoski M.J., & Robins C.J., 'Effects of mindfulness on psychological health: a review of empirical studies'. *Clinical Psychology Review.* 31(6): 1041–56, Aug 2011.

Kirk, Alana, *Midlife, Redefined.* Dancer Publishing, 2022.

Kirk, Alana, *The Sandwich Years.* Hachette Books Ireland, 2016.

Li, Q., Nakadai, A., Matsushima, H., *et al.* 'Phytoncides (wood essential oils) induce human natural killer cell activity'. *Immunopharmacology and Immunotoxicology.* 28(2): 319–33, 2006.

Mehta, Saznin, 'Building the Good Life: Finding Meaning and Purpose to Achieve Well-Being'. Johns Hopkins, Bloomberg School of Public Health, 2025.

Neff, Kristen, *Self-Compassion: Stop Beating Yourself Up and Leave Insecurity Behind.* William Morrow & Co, 2011.

Nestor, James, *Breath: The New Science of a Lost Art.* Penguin Life, 2020.

NHS: https://www.nhs.uk/live-well/eat-well/food-types/different-fats-nutrition/#:~:text=A%20small%20amount%20of%20fat,with%20the%20help%20of%20fats.

O'Murchú, Niall, The Blissful Breath Academy. www.breathewithniall.com.

Orbinski, Niamh, *No Apologies,* Harper Collins, 2023.

Patel, A., Schofield, G.M., Kolt, G.S. *et al.*, 'General practitioners views and experiences of counselling for physical activity through the New Zealand Green Prescription program'. *BMC Fam Pract*, 12, 119, 2011. https://bmcprimcare.biomedcentral.com/articles/10.1186.1471-2296-12-119.

Ramage, Andy, *Let's Do This!: How to Use Motivational Psychology to Change Your Habits for Life*. Astor, 2019.

Rensselaer Polytechnic Institute, 'Minority rules: Scientists discover tipping point for the spread of ideas'. *ScienceDaily*, 26 July 2011.

Saskatchewan Blue Cross: https://www.sk.bluecross.ca/advice-centre/blog/the-basics-of-building-a-balanced-plate-dietitians-4-step-formula-nutrition-month-2023.

Senninger T., *Abenteuer leiten in abenteuern lernen*. Aachen: OEkotopia, 2000.

Smith, Chris, *Don't Die*, Netflix, 2025.

Smith, Niamh, Georgiou, Michail, King, Abby C., Tieges, Zoë, Webb, Stephen & Chastin, Sebastien, 'Urban blue spaces and human health: A systematic review and meta-analysis of quantitative studies'. *Cities*, Volume 119, 2021.

Stunkard, Albert *et al.*, 'The Results of treatment for obesity; a review of the literature and report of a series'. AMA *Archives of Internal Medicine*. 103(1) January 1959.

Tolle, Eckhart, *The Power of Now*. Namaste Publishing, 1997.

Tribole, Evelyn, & Resch, Elyse, *Intuitive Eating*, St. Martin's Essentials, 2020.

Wedesweiler, Madeleine, 'The 10,000 steps a day idea was made up by a clock company. How many should you take?'. *SBS News*. 2023.

Wexner Medical Centre: https://wexnermedical.osu.edu/our-stories/boost-your-brain-power-with-the-right-nutrition#:~:text='%20Did%20you%20know%20up%20to,important%20for%20learning%20and%20memory.

Williamson, Marianne, *A Return to Love*. HarperCollins,1992.

Wolf, Naomi, *The Beauty Myth: How Images of Beauty Are Used Against Women*. Chatto & Windus, 1990.

ACKNOWLEDGEMENTS

I am very lucky to be surrounded by great people in my life, and I am so grateful for all of them. To my mum Anne, my sister Nuala and my brother Paul, forever my favourites, I love how we love, I love how we laugh and I love how we talk about everything. The way we came together to care for Dad in his final years will always mean the world to me.

I've made room for more favourites with a family of my own now. To my husband Jonathan/Ronnie, having two names makes it seem to strangers that I have two men on the go, but I only need one and that is you. I adore you and thank you for the beautiful life we have together. To my children Flynn and Lois, watching you grow into the gorgeous people you are now has been one of my best life experiences. I want you both to fly but hope we will always be close, we are so proud of you both.

I have a great extended family, and I lucked out with my in laws, they all mean so much to me but I'm going to dangerously mention one – Auntie Nuala, so special to us all, thank you for being you.

To my friends, for lighting up my life, thank you! My dad once told me that one of his favourite qualities in a person is that they laugh easily and I must have that in my DNA, all of my friends are up for fun, make me laugh and allow me to be the messer that I am. They are also always there for the ups and the downs. I'm so lucky I get to have you all in my life.

To my on-air family from jobs current and past, I have been lucky to work with some incredible people in front and behind the scenes in radio and TV. I'll always be grateful for the fun I've had at 'work' and every opportunity that came my way.

To all the lovely people who listen to my podcasts, my radio show on Newstalk or who have taken the time over the years to come to my events, send me a message on Instagram or say hi and that they like what I do, I never take that for granted. Likewise, to anyone who has trusted me with their life story and allowed me to help them tell it to a listening audience, thank you.

To the people who have shaped me and taught me so much, many of whom are mentioned in this book. Josie and Níall O'Murchú and all my fellow teachers at the Blissful Breathwork Academy, Judith McAdam, Aidan O'Brien, Aisling Nestor,

Oonagh O'Hagan, The Institute of Integrative Nutrition, Daniel Davey and the many people who I have interviewed who have all taught me from their expertise and experience.

To the people of the wellness world that I now exist within, how lucky am I? I get to mix with great people, many of whom have become friends for life, and I get to learn how to live life better from your wisdom. I am very grateful to you all. It's great to have meditation specialists, neuroscientists, sound-bath practitioners, therapists, yogis and nutritionists on speed dial!

To the team at Hachette for giving me this opportunity – to Ciara Doorley, my editor, for her faith in me, the enthusiasm with each read and her gently nudging the project along. To Stephen, Chloe, Elaine and all the team, thanks for your valuable input.

To James and Bryan of TedX Tralee – giving me a spot on that stage led to this book deal so thank you, that weekend is the gift that keeps on giving.

To Lynn, Aoifa, Natalie and all at Collab Agency for representing and hooking a girl up so well.

And to you the reader, thanks for picking this book up and giving it a go. I truly hope it's shifted or reset how you feel about your wellbeing.